Bed & Breakfast
Southern California

Automobile Club of Southern California

Writer............................Michael Lugenbuehl
Artist.............................Virginia Matijevac
Editorial Assistant............Andrea Canfield
Editor............................Kristine Miller

Information presented in this publication has been carefully researched and was as accurate as possible at press time, but the Automobile Club of Southern California is not responsible for any changes or errors which may occur. It is wise to verify information before your visit.

ISBN: **1-56413-458-X**
Printed in the United States of America

Table of Contents

Bed and Breakfast Inns

Bed and breakfast establishments today flourish throughout the United States as delightful alternatives to traditional motel or hotel lodging. The promise of warm hospitality, distinctive architecture or decor and the chance to mingle with fellow travelers lures the businessperson as well as the vacationer.

B&Bs can be found throughout much of Southern California. They offer a wide variety of settings and atmospheres. Many are original Victorian, Queen Anne or Craftsman houses filled with antiques and echoes of an earlier era. Others are of more recent vintage but still evoke the past with Early American, country or farmhouse-style furnishings. Occasionally even a log house, mountain cabin or beachfront cottage can be found. In those instances when an establishment is described as "contemporary," it does not necessarily refer to the style of architecture; in most contexts it means the building is of recent construction, generally within the last 20 or 30 years. Some houses were built specifically to be a bed and breakfast establishment.

Bed and breakfast homes are often "better" than home because the service includes breakfast (you don't have to cook or do the dishes) and maid service (you don't have to make your bed or vacuum). A continental breakfast typically consists of homemade muffins or fancy breads, juice and coffee; many establishments provide an "expanded continental" breakfast, adding fresh fruits, cheeses and cold cereals to the spread. A full breakfast includes eggs or another cooked entree. In pleasant weather, breakfast might be served in the patio or garden. B&B guests usually eat together, giving them a chance to meet and share experiences.

Amenities vary with each B&B. Some provide a cup of tea, glass of wine or other refreshment in the afternoon or evening. Occasionally establishments have pianos, and guests may be invited to play for their own enjoyment or for the entertainment of others. Those with lawns may have chairs or benches that invite guests to sit and observe the area's birds or scenic beauty. Some B&Bs offer easy access to hiking trails or bicycle paths, and a few even provide the use of bicycles. Some inns also have swimming pools or whirlpools for their guests' pleasure. When the bed and breakfast happens to be on the coast, a walk along the beach is an added bonus.

Many people find that the B&B setting makes an ideal place to spend a honeymoon or a romantic weekend. Breakfast might be served in the room. Some innkeepers will even oblige with breakfast in bed. Many rooms are equipped with fireplaces or whirlpools.

Generally B&Bs contain from three to 16 guest rooms, most with private baths. Many older houses feature old-fashioned footed bathtubs, but modern conveniences are not forgotten; these tubs usually are equipped with showers and possibly a terry robe. Of course all inns have telephones, but often no phones ring in the guest rooms. A few houses provide data ports for those who can't leave the computer behind. Some houses offer television sets in each room, but most have only one television in the living or common room (a few places don't have any at all). In addition to watching television, the common room may be used for reading, conversation with other guests, or just relaxing.

Bed and breakfast inns thrive throughout Southern California. Some are located in the heart of major cities, such as Los Angeles and San Diego; others are tucked away in small towns like Cambria or Julian. Several B&Bs can be found in the mountains at Big Bear and Lake Arrowhead, as well as near the ocean in Avalon or Newport Beach. Some B&Bs offer proximity to national parks such as Joshua Tree National Park and Sequoia and Kings National Parks.

These inns are the perfect place to escape from the hustle and bustle of modern living. With such a wide variety of locations and atmospheres to choose from, there's bound to be a bed and breakfast for everyone. To help in the selection, this book provides an overview of B&B establishments in Southern California, listed alphabetically by city. A map showing general locations of these B&Bs can be found on pages 10 and 11. Detailed locations can be found on Auto Club of Southern California county and city maps, sold through selected booksellers throughout Southern California and available at no charge to members in Auto Club District Offices.

Room Rates

Published rates were submitted by each bed and breakfast inn's management. Rates are generally shown for one person (1P), two persons with one bed (2P/1B) and two persons with two beds (2P/2B); rates for full-cabin rentals or other special units are also listed where applicable.

Where available, the rate for each additional person (XP) is also provided. **All rates shown are subject to change**. Major credit cards honored by establishments are abbreviated as follows: AE=American Express; CB=Carte Blanche; DI=Diners Club; DS=Discover; JCB=Japanese Credit Bureau; MC=MasterCard; VI=VISA.

Points to Consider

The appeal of bed and breakfast inns lies in their individuality and their diversity. Each has its own character, history and atmosphere. In order to maintain these qualities, inns may have certain restrictions, and you should be sure to ask about any that might affect you. The following are some of the points that should be considered when booking a reservation.

- In most cases **pets** should stay home. While some pets travel well, they often become nervous in unfamiliar surroundings. Damage to antique furnishings, imported rugs or carpeting can bring an expensive end to an otherwise pleasant stay. Also, some inns have resident cats or dogs; this may be a consideration for guests with allergies or those who are unaccustomed to pets.

- At most inns **smoking** is allowed only on an outside porch or patio. Some establishments do allow cigarette smoking in specific rooms.

- Innkeepers prefer that guests leave **valuables** at home. It is unwise to leave expensive camera equipment, jewelry or other valuables in the room. On occasion the house may be unattended, and, unlike hotels, there is rarely a safe for storing valuables.

- All bed and breakfast inns listed here are **inspected** periodically by representatives of the Auto Club. These inns are clean and well maintained, but more emphasis is placed on atmosphere—style of operation—than on the nature of appointments. For instance, rooms don't always have private baths or easy chairs.

- Guests should be prepared to transport their own baggage between their car and room, and to attend to their own personal needs during their stay. While hotels hire staff specifically to perform such services, B&Bs do not, and innkeepers should not be expected to act as **porters** or to be constantly on call.

8

- **Soundproofing** is not always up to the same standards as in a hotel. Noises from the kitchen and elsewhere can sometimes be heard in the guest rooms.

- Off-street **parking** is not always available. It may be necessary to park your car along the street.

- B&B guests are exactly that—guests—and as such should exhibit the same **behavior** as if in the home of a respected friend.

Making Reservations

Reservations at bed and breakfast inns are essential and should be made well in advance. Because each inn has different amenities and may have restrictions that might affect you, it is important to ask about these when making a reservation. The Automobile Club of Southern California will make a reservation for AAA members at any of the inns listed in this book. At most establishments, advance deposits are required. Cancellation refund policies vary, and minimum-stay requirements may be in effect, usually during weekends and holidays.

When a reservation is made, the innkeeper should be notified of the expected arrival time of the guest.

> *Effective August 14, 1999, portions*
> *of area code 805 will change to 661;*
> *effective June 10, 2000, the eastern portions*
> *of area code 619 will change to 935;*
> *as of press deadline, those telephone*
> *numbers known to be affected are*
> *listed with both area codes.*

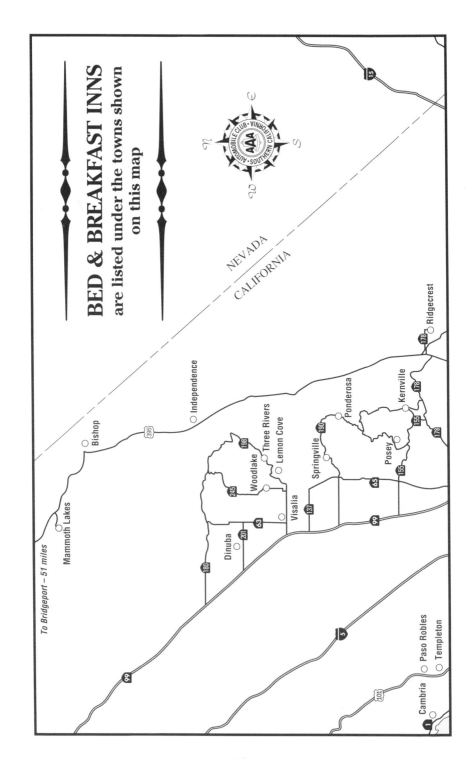

BED & BREAKFAST INNS
are listed under the towns shown
on this map

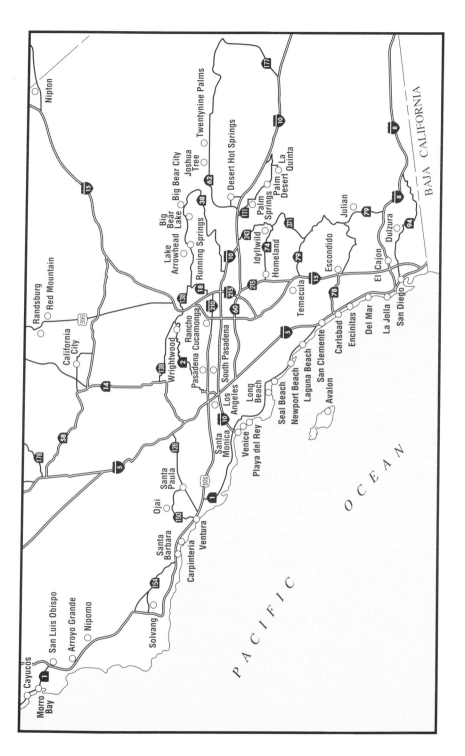

Bed & Breakfast Listings

🐾 ARROYO GRANDE

CRYSTAL ROSE INN
(805) 481-1854, (800) 707-3466
789 Valley Rd, 93420.

1P/1B $ 95 - 185	2P/1B $ 95 - 185	2P/2B $ 85 - 175

XP $35. 2 pm check-in; 11 am check out. 7-day refund notice. Midweek package.

This 1890 Victorian mansion on 1½ acres of gardens is located in a rural area. 8 rooms, each with private bath. In-room phones. Bicycles, croquet, volleyball, badminton, horseshoes, boccie ball and exercise room. No pets. Meeting rooms. AE, DS, MC, VI. Full breakfast served in guest room or garden. High tea and light lunch served in the afternoon; hors d'oeuvres and wine served in the evening. Dinner and full bar service may be purchased in a restaurant on the premises. Smoking in gardens only.

THE GRIEB FARMHOUSE INN
(805) 481-8540
851 Todd Ln, 93420-3912.

1P/1B $ 75	2P/1B $ 85

3 pm check-in; 11 am check out. 2-night minimum stay weekends and holidays. Deposit required; 2-day refund notice. Cash or check only.

An 1888 Victorian farmhouse with a wraparound porch has a country theme, hardwood floors and antique furniture. One mile from the Old Village of Arroyo Grande. 2 guest rooms, each with private bath. Coffee served in the hallway. No pets. Full breakfast served in the dining room. Evening snacks and beverages. No smoking.

THE GUEST HOUSE
(805) 481-9304
Located in Arroyo Grande Village at 120 Hart Ln, 93420.

1P/1B $ 50	2P/1B $ 70

XP $15. No specified check-in or check out times. Deposit required; 36-hour refund notice.

New England Colonial-style house with antique furnishings is set among old-fashioned gardens. 2 guest rooms with 1 shared bath. Full breakfast served in the parlor or on the terrace. Beverages served in the afternoon. No pets; 2 resident cats. Smoking in public rooms only.

HOUSE OF ANOTHER TYME BED & BREAKFAST   *(805) 489-6313;*
227 Le Point St, 93421.   *FAX (805) 489-6313*

1P/1B $ 95   2P/1B $ 95

3 pm check-in; 11 am check out. 2-night minimum stay holiday weekends. Deposit required; 3-day refund notice.

A 1916 single-wall construction house on ¼ acre is furnished with antiques. One block up a hill from the Village of Arroyo Grande. 3 guest rooms, each with private bath. No pets. DS, MC, VI. Full country breakfast served in dining area or garden area. Evening cookies or pastry with coffee, tea or punch. Smoking outside only.

❦ AVALON

THE OLD TURNER INN   *(310) 510-2236*
232 Catalina Ave; Box 97, 90704.

1P/1B   ...   2P/1B $120 - 200

XP $30. 2 pm check-in; 11 am check out. 2-night minimum stay most weekends. Reservation required; 7-day refund notice; cancellation fee.

A 1927 Cape Cod-style house with a large brick fireplace, grand piano and an enclosed sitting porch is decorated in a casual, classic-country decor. Located 1 block from the bay. 5 guest rooms, each with private bath; 4 with fireplace. In-room TV. Bicycles available for guests' use. No pets. DS, MC, VI. Expanded continental breakfast. Smoking not permitted.

❦ BIG BEAR CITY

GOLD MOUNTAIN MANOR HISTORIC BED & BREAKFAST
(909) 585-6997, (800) 509-2604; FAX (909) 585-0327
1117 Anita Ave; Box 2027, 92314.

1P/1B   ...   2P/1B $125 - 190

2-9 pm check-in; noon check out. In-season 2-night minimum stay weekends, 3 nights required on holidays. Credit card guarantee; 7-day refund notice. Off-season and midweek discounts.

A 1931 log mountain mansion is decorated with antique furnishings. Located near the San Bernardino National Forest. 4 guest rooms and 2 suites, each with private bath and fireplace. Game room with pool table. No pets. MC, VI. Full breakfast served in the dining room or on the veranda. Hors d'oeuvres served in the afternoon. Smoking outside only.

❦ BIG BEAR LAKE

ALPENHORN BED & BREAKFAST   *(909) 866-5700;*
601 Knight Ave, 92315.   *reservations (888) 829-6600; FAX (909) 878-3209*

1P/1B $ 75 - 160   2P/1B $ 95 - 175

XP $25. 3 pm check-in; 11 am check out. 2-night minimum stay weekends and holidays. Deposit required; 5-day refund notice. Midweek rates.

A contemporary mountain lodge is located in a quiet residential neighborhood between shops and a ski resort. 7 rooms, each with private bath, whirlpool tub, fireplace, TV/VCR and phone; 6 rooms have balconies. No pets. MC, VI. Full gourmet breakfast served in the dining room. Complimentary wine and hors d'oeuvres served in the evening. No smoking.

APPLES BED AND BREAKFAST INN   *(909) 866-0903*
42430 Moonridge Rd, 92315.

1P/1B $145 - 185   2P/1B $145 - 185

2 pm check-in; noon check out. 2-night minimum stay weekends, longer during major holidays. Deposit required; 7-day refund notice, 14 days during holiday periods. Midweek rates.

Contemporary Victorian-style home is set in an acre of pine. Rooms individually decorated. 12 guest rooms, each with private bath; 4 with whirlpool tubs for 2. In-room gas fireplace, TV, VCR. The large gathering room has a wood-burning stove, game table, baby grand piano and library loft. No pets. AE, DS, MC, VI. Full breakfast served in the dining area. Refreshment bar available all day. Sparkling cider and appetizers served in the afternoon, desserts in the evening. Smoking outside only.

EAGLE'S NEST BED & BREAKFAST　　　*(909) 866-6465, (888) 866-6465*
41675 Big Bear Blvd; Box 1003, 92315.

1P/1B 　$ 85 - 170 　　　　2P/1B 　$ 85 - 170

2 pm check-in; 11 am check out. 2-night minimum stay weekends. Deposit required; 5-day refund notice. Off-season and midweek rates.

Contemporary log lodge with country antiques is surrounded by tall pines. 10 guest rooms, each with private bath. Units available with TV, whirlpool and fireplace. Pets allowed in 1 unit. AE, DS, MC, VI. Full breakfast served in the dining room or brought to the guest room. Complimentary hors d'oeuvres in the evening. Some units available for smokers.

THE INN AT FAWNSKIN　　　*(909) 866-3200, (888) 329-6754*
880 Canyon Dr, Fawnskin 92333.

1P/1B 　$ 75 - 165 　　　　2P/1B 　$ 85 - 175

XP $10. 3 pm check-in; noon check out. 2-night minimum stay weekends. Deposit required; 10-day refund notice, 30 days during holiday periods; cancellation fee. Midweek rates.

Located near the village of Fawnskin on the north shore of Big Bear Lake, this log house has interior pine walls and country decor. 4 rooms, 2 with private bath. 3 rooms accommodate 2 persons; the suite can hold 4. 1 room with TV and fireplace. No pets. MC, VI. Full breakfast served in the dining room. Beverages and hors d'oeuvres served in the afternoon. Smoking outside only.

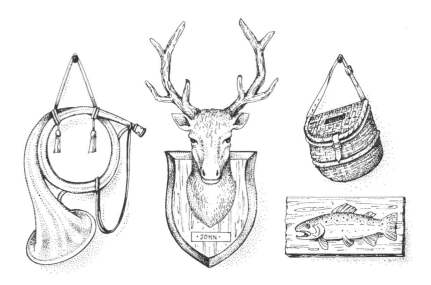

SWITZERLAND HAUS BED & BREAKFAST   *(909) 866-3729, (800) 335-3729*
41829 Switzerland Dr, 92315.

1P/1B   ...   2P/1B $125 - 175

XP $20. 2 pm check-in; noon check out. 2-night minimum stay weekends. Credit card guarantee required; 7-day refund notice. Off-season rates.

A Swiss-style house is located near Snow Summit Ski Area in the San Bernardino Mountains. 4 rooms and a suite, each with private bath. In-room TV, VCR. Suite has fireplace, refrigerator, microwave, coffeemaker and view of the ski slopes. No pets. AE, DS, MC, VI. Full breakfast served in the dining area. Hot and cold drinks and snacks available all day; evening desserts served. Smoking outside only.

TRUFFLES BED & BREAKFAST   *Phone & FAX (909) 585-2772;*
43591 Bow Canyon Rd; Box 130649, 92315.   *Phone (800) 697-9352*

1P/1B $115 - 150   2P/1B $115 - 150

2:30 pm check-in; 11:30 am check out. 2-night minimum stay holidays. Deposit required; 7-day refund notice; $10 cancellation fee.

Country manor-style house with dormers is located near Bear Mountain Ski Area and Golf Course. The house has a large rock fireplace and sitting area; common room with TV, VCR and movies; deck with view of Bear Mountain. Reading/library room, exercise room, gift shop. 5 guest rooms, each with private bath. In-room TV. No pets. Facilities for weddings and small conferences. AE, DS, MC, VI. Full breakfast served in the dining room. Evening desserts with home-baked pastries, coffee and soft drinks; truffles on guests' pillows. Occasional afternoon teas. No smoking.

WINDY POINT INN   *(909) 866-2746; FAX (909) 866-1593*
39015 North Shore Dr; Box 375, Fawnskin 92333.

1P/1B   ...   2P/1B $135 - 245

3 pm check-in; noon check out. 2-night minimum stay holidays and weekends. Deposit required; 7-day refund notice. Midweek rates.

Contemporary lakefront lodge situated on a private point overlooking the lake is bounded by 2 secluded, sandy beaches. The lodge is decorated with a collection of antiques blended with contemporary furnishings. 5 guest rooms, each with private bath; 4 with whirlpool tub, 1 with bidet and steam sauna. In-room fireplace, refrigerator, ceiling fan, stereo cassette player and private deck. Whirlpool. No pets. AE, DS, MC, VI. Full breakfast served in a separate dining area. Refreshments served in the afternoon. No smoking.

🍎 BISHOP

THE CHALFANT HOUSE
213 Academy St, 93514.

(760) 872-1790

| 1P/1B | $ 50 | 2P/1B | $ 60 - 100 | 2P/2B | $ 70 |

3 pm check-in; 11 am check out. Deposit required; 24-hour refund notice.

A turn-of-the-century, semi-Victorian-style 2-story house includes country antique furnishings and features handmade quilts. 5 rooms and 3 suites, each with private bath. TV, VCR and fireplace in the parlor. Central air conditioning; in-room phones available. No pets. AE, DS, MC, VI. Full breakfast served in the dining room. Tea served in the afternoon; ice cream sundaes served in the evening. No smoking.

THE MATLICK HOUSE
1313 Rowan Ln, 93514.

(760) 873-3133, (800) 898-3133

| 1P/1B | ... | 2P/1B | $ 75 - 85 |

3 pm check-in; 11 am check out. Deposit required; 7-day refund notice.

A 1906 two-story ranch house decorated with antique furnishings lies 1 mile north of town, in a rural setting. 5 rooms, each with private bath. Air conditioning; all rooms have a telephone jack. No pets. Full breakfast served in the dining area. Wine and hors d'oeuvres served in the evening on the veranda or in the parlor. Smoking permitted on the veranda only.

🐝 BRIDGEPORT

THE CAIN HOUSE   *(760) 932-7040, (800) 433-2246; FAX (760) 932-7419*
340 Main St; Box 454, 93517.

1P/1B $ 80 - 135   2P/1B $ 80 - 135

3 pm check-in; 11 am check out. 2-night minimum stay during holidays and special event weekends. Deposit required; 2-day refund notice.

A 1930s historic wood-sided house in the shadow of the Eastern Sierra features papered walls complementing European country-style furnishings. 7 guest rooms, each with private bath. In-room TV; in-room phone available. No pets. AE, CB, DI, DS, MC, VI. Full breakfast served in the dining area. Wine and cheese available 5-7 pm. No smoking.

🐝 CALIFORNIA CITY

RANCH CONCHITA   *(760) 373-2198, 373-2610*
14 miles N at end of Lake Rd; Box 1616, Cantil 93519.

1P/1B ...   2P/1B $ 75   2P/2B $ 75

XP $5. A group of 6 couples can be accommodated at reduced rates in a cabin on adjacent ranch. 2-night minimum stay holiday weekends. Deposit required; cancellation fee.

A California ranch house with country decor has extensive views of Mojave Desert scenery. 6 rooms, 3 with private bath. In-room phone and TV by prior arrangement. Pool, game room and common room with fireplace for guests. Bird-watching, duck hunting in season. No pets; stables available if guests arrange to bring their own horses. MC, VI. Expanded continental breakfast in a basket served in guest room; visitors may also take breakfast to courtyard or garden. Tea and sodas served in afternoon or evening. Other meals can be ordered at an additional charge. Smoking outside only.

❤ CAMBRIA

BEACH HOUSE
(805) 927-3136
6360 Moonstone Beach Dr, 93428.

1P/1B   ...   2P/1B $130 - 165

3 pm check-in; 11 am check out. 2-night minimum stay holiday weekends. Deposit required; 7-day refund notice.

3-story oceanfront house decorated with traditional and antique furnishings features a large fireplace in the common room. Guest rooms have ocean views. 7 guest rooms, each with private bath. In-room TV. Patios and decks with beach furniture. No pets. MC, VI. Full breakfast served at the family's restaurant 6 doors away, which features oceanfront dining. Complimentary wine with cheese and crackers. Smoking outside only.

BLUE WHALE INN
(805) 927-4647
6736 Moonstone Beach Dr, 93428.

1P/1B $155 - 220   2P/1B $155 - 220

2 pm check-in; 11 am check out. 2-night minimum stay weekends. Deposit required; 10-day refund notice.

Contemporary Cape Cod-style inn has European country decor and an oceanfront location. Guest rooms have a private entrance and an ocean view. 6 rooms, each with private bath. Canopy beds. In-room TV, gas fireplace and phone. No pets. MC, VI. Full breakfast served in the dining area. Refreshments served in the afternoon. Smoking outside only.

THE J. PATRICK HOUSE
(805) 927-3812, (800) 341-5258;
FAX (805) 927-6759

2990 Burton Dr, 93428.

1P/1B   ...   2P/1B $125 - 180

3 pm check-in; 11 am check out. 2-night minimum stay weekends. Deposit required; 7-day refund notice.

Early American log cabin-style inn is situated in the woods above the East Village area of town. 8 guest rooms, each with private bath; 1 room in the main cabin house, and 7 rooms in the Carriage House accessed through the garden; all rooms have wood-burning fireplace or stove. No pets. AE, DS, MC, VI. Full breakfast served in the garden room. Beverages and appetizers served at 5:30 pm. No smoking.

OLALLIEBERRY INN   *(805) 927-3222, (888) 927-3222; FAX (805) 927-0202*
2476 Main St, 93428.

1P/1B   ...   2P/1B $ 90 - 185

XP $20. 3-7 pm check-in; 11 am check out. Deposit required; 7-day refund notice.

Registered, historic 1873 Greek Revival house and cottage with garden overlook Santa Rosa Creek and are decorated with period antiques. 9 guest rooms, each with private bath; 6 with gas/log fireplace. Butterfly and herb gardens, and a 110-year-old redwood grace the front yard. Located within walking distance of restaurants and shops. No pets. AE, MC, VI. Full breakfast is served in the dining area; complimentary wine and afternoon hors d'oeuvres. Smoking outside only.

THE SQUIBB HOUSE   *(805) 927-9600*
4063 Burton Dr, 93428.

1P/1B $ 95 - 140   2P/1B $ 95 - 140

3 pm check-in; 11 am check out. 2-night minimum stay weekends and holidays. Deposit required; 7-day refund notice; $20 cancellation fee.

Built in 1877, this Victorian-style residence touts beautiful gardens and a gazebo, and has been designated a State Historic Site. 5 rooms, each with fireplace and private bath. Expanded continental breakfast served in guest rooms or separate dining area. Complimentary wine tasting at tasting room across the street. Located within walking distance of restaurants, shops and galleries. No pets. AE, MC, VI. Smoking not permitted.

❦ CARLSBAD

PELICAN COVE BED & BREAKFAST INN   *(760) 434-5995, (888) 735-2683*
320 Walnut Ave, 92008.

1P/1B $ 85 - 175   2P/1B $ 90 - 180   2P/2B $ 90 - 180

XP $15. 3 pm check-in; 11 am check out. 2-night minimum stay weekends. Deposit required; 7-day refund notice.

Contemporary Cape Cod-style inn is located 2 blocks from the beach. 8 guest rooms, each with private bath. In-room TV, radio and gas fireplace. 2 rooms with whirlpool. AE, MC, VI. Full breakfast served in the dining room. No smoking.

❧ CARPINTERIA

PRUFROCK'S GARDEN INN   *(805) 566-9696, (888) 778-3765*
600 Linden Ave, 93013.

1P/1B $ 99 - 229   2P/1B $ 99 - 229

XP $25. 4 pm check-in; 11 am check out. 2-night minimum stay weekends. Deposit required; 7-day refund notice, $15 cancellation fee. Midweek rates.

Renovated historic California cottage-style house, built in 1904 has colorful flower gardens. Located on the town's main street, it is 4 blocks from the beach. 7 guest rooms, 5 with private bath. No pets. DI, MC, VI. Full breakfast. Sunset hors d'oeuvres. No smoking.

❧ CATALINA ISLAND (SEE AVALON)

❧ CAYUCOS

THE VICTORIAN ROSE GARDEN BED & BREAKFAST   *(805) 995-3382*
391 D St, 93430.

1P/1B $110 - 150   2P/1B $125 - 175

XP $25. 2 pm check-in; 11 am check out. 2-night minimum stay weekends and holidays. 7-day refund notice.

Century-old Victorian home surrounded by 80 rose bushes is just a few blocks from the beach. Guest rooms have antiques and stained glass windows. 3 guest rooms, 1 with private bath. In-room TV and VCR. Parlor with fireplace. Outdoor hot tub enclosed in original barn. No pets. MC, VI. Full gourmet breakfast served in the dining area. Vegetarian breakfast available on request. Early morning coffee or tea delivered to the room. Complimentary evening appetizers. No smoking.

❧ DEL MAR

THE BLUE DOOR   *(858) 755-3819*
13707 Durango Dr, 92014.

1P/1B   ...   2P/1B $ 70 - 80

3 pm check-in; noon check out. Deposit required; 2-day refund notice.

New England-style house is located near Torrey Pines State Reserve and the coast. 1 suite with private bath. No pets. Full breakfast served in the dining area. No smoking.

❦ DESERT HOT SPRINGS

TRAVELLERS REPOSE BED & BREAKFAST   *(760) 329-9584*
66920 1st St; Box 655, 92240.

1P/1B   ...   2P/1B $ 65 - 85

Closed Jul and Aug. 2-6 pm check-in; 11 am check out. Deposit required; 10-day refund notice.

Contemporary, 2-story Victorian-style house. 3 guest rooms, each with private bath. Hot tub. No pets. Expanded continental breakfast served in the dining area or on the patio. Tea served at 4 pm. Smoking outside only.

❦ DINUBA

REEDLEY COUNTRY INN   *(559) 638-2585, (559) 638-3445;*
43137 Rd 52, Reedley 93654.   *FAX (559) 638-8099*

1P/1B   ...   2P/1B $ 75 - 95

XP $15. 3 pm check-in; 11:30 am check out. Deposit required; 3-day refund notice.

Restored 1908 Tudor house is set in a fruit orchard on a working plum farm. The grounds feature lush gardens with hundreds of roses, a gazebo and patio. 4 guest rooms and 1 suite, each with private bath. In-room air conditioning, phone, TV; 2 rooms with whirlpool tub. No pets. AE, MC, VI. Full breakfast served in the dining area. Afternoon snacks available. Complimentary fruit available in summer and fall. Smoking outside only.

❦ DULZURA

BROOKSIDE FARM BED AND BREAKFAST INN   *(619/935) 468-3043*
1373 Marron Valley Rd, 91917.

1P/1B   ...   2P/1B $ 85 - 120

3 pm check-in; 11 am check out. 2-night minimum stay required in some rooms on weekends. Deposit required; 7-day refund notice.

A 1928 farmhouse located next to a brook in a rural mountain valley has extensive and varied gardens; the interior features antique furnishings. 9 guest rooms and 1 cabin, each with private bath. Hot tub. No pets. Full breakfast served in the dining area. Complimentary supper served in the dining area Sun through Thu. Gourmet dinner available on weekends by prior arrangement; extra charge. Smoking outside only.

🍎 EL CAJON

AT YOUR LEISURE BED AND BREAKFAST   *(619/935) 444-3124*
525 S 3rd St, 92019.

| 1P/1B $ 65 | 2P/1B $ 68 | 2P/2B $ 68 |

XP $8. No specified check-in or check out times. Deposit required.

Historic 1928 Craftsman farmhouse has a large front porch with swing and a back patio with pool. Located a short distance from I-8 (2nd St exit); also close to bus and trolley lines. 2 guest rooms with shared bath. In-room air conditioning and TV. No pets. MC, VI. Expanded continental breakfast served in the dining room. Smoking permitted outside only.

🍎 ENCINITAS

SEA BREEZE BED & BREAKFAST INN   *(760) 944-0318*
121 Vulcan Ave, 92024.

| 1P/1B $ 60 | 2P/1B $ 75 | 2P/Suite $ 90 |
| 2P/Penthouse $ 150 | 2P/Apartment $ 150 | |

XP $10. 2-7 pm check-in; noon check out. 2-night minimum stay weekends and holidays. Deposit required; 7-day refund notice, $10 cancellation fee.

Contemporary 2-story house with ocean view features handcrafted decor. 3 guest rooms, a 1-bedroom kitchen apartment and a penthouse with whirlpool tub, each with private bath and separate entrance. In-room phone and cable TV. Gas fireplace in the common sitting area and in the apartment. No pets. DS, MC, VI. Specialty muffins are included in the expanded continental breakfast, served in the dining area or on the patio. Wine and cheese served during the afternoon social hour. Smoking permitted with restrictions.

❦ ESCONDIDO

LAKE HODGES HOUSE
3443 Via Loma Vista, 92029.

(760) 747-9626; FAX (760) 747-3331

1P/1B $145   2P/2B $145

1:30 pm check-in; 11 am check out. Deposit required; 7-day refund notice, 14 days for holidays.

The house is located in a custom residential, semirural district overlooking the lake. 2 rooms, each with private bath. In-room phone. Pool, whirlpool, bicycles, library/music center. No pets; outdoor resident cats. MC, VI. Full breakfast served in dining room or patio. Champagne, juice, fruit, cheese and other snacks are in room. Smoking outside only.

ZOSA GARDENS & RANCH BED & BREAKFAST
9381 W Lilac Rd, 92026.

(800) 711-8361

1P/1B $135 - 195   2P/1B $135 - 195

XP $20. 2 pm check-in, noon check out. Credit card guarantee required; cancellation fee. Lower rates during off season.

The hacienda-style house is located minutes from the wine country and Temecula. The grounds have fruit trees and flower fields. 9 rooms and a 2-bedroom cottage; all have private bath. Cottage is in an avocado grove. In-room air conditioning, fireplaces, 1 room with TV. Pool, hot tub, tennis courts, game room. No pets. AE, DI, DS, MC, VI. Full breakfast is by the pool or in a separate serving room. Wine and hors d'oeuvres served 4-5:30 pm. Smoking outside only. Handicap accessible.

🍎 HOMELAND

PIERSON'S COUNTRY PLACE

(909) 926-4546; FAX (909) 926-1456

25185 Pierson Rd, 92548.

1P/1B $ 85 - 125   2P/1B $ 85 - 125

3 pm check-in; 11 am check out. Deposit required. 5-day refund notice.

This 6500-square-foot Mediterranean-style home is 20 miles north of the Temecula wine country. Each guest room has an individual decorative theme. 5 guest rooms, each with private bath. Secluded outside spa. Pool table, piano, card table, fireplace in living room. MC, VI. Full breakfast served on patio or in dining area. Hors d'oeuvres and beverages served in the evening. Smoking in spa area only.

RANCHO KAERU BED & BREAKFAST

(909) 926-5133;
reservations (714) 894-5635; FAX (714) 891-4035

24180 Juniper Flats Rd, 92548.

1P/1B $ 75   2P/1B $ 85

No specified check-in or check out times. $10 surcharge for a 1-night stay. Deposit required; 3-day refund notice.

A 1935 replica of a historic French country stone house sits on 20 acres in a rural area with flowers, ponds and a spring. It is decorated with antique furnishings. 2 rooms, each with private bath. In-room fireplace. No pets. Full gourmet breakfast served in the dining area. No smoking.

🍏 IDYLLWILD

CREEKSTONE INN—BED & BREAKFAST   *(909) 659-3342, (800) 409-2127*
54950 Pine Crest Ave, 92549.

1P/1B   ...   2P/1B $ 95 - 145

3 pm check-in; 11 am check out. 2-night minimum stay weekends; 3 nights required on some holidays. Deposit required; 14-day refund notice.

Local stone masons built this unique alpine-style house in 1942 using massive river stones. A large stone fireplace and antique furnishings highlight the interior. 9 guest rooms, each with private bath; 7 with fireplace; some with whirlpool tub. No pets. MC, VI. Full breakfast served in dining area. Smoking outside only.

THE PINE COVE INN   *(909) 659-5033, (888) 659-5033;*
23481 SR 243; Box 2181, 92549.   *FAX (909) 659-5034*

1P/1B   ...   2P/1B $ 70 - 100   2P/2B $ 70 - 100

XP $10. 1-7 pm check-in; noon check out. 2-night minimum stay weekends, 3 nights required on holidays. Deposit required; 2-day refund notice.

A 1935 rustic main lodge and three adjacent A-frame cabins are located 3 miles north of town in Pine Cove. 9 guest rooms, each with private bath. 3 rooms with wood fireplace; 3 with electric fireplace. In-room refrigerator and microwave; 1 unit with TV, kitchen and separate living room. Conference room. No pets. AE, DS, MC, VI. Full breakfast served in the lodge. Smoking in some units and lodge.

STRAWBERRY CREEK INN   *(909) 659-3202, (800) 262-8969*
26370 SR 243; Box 1818, 92549.

1P/1B   ...   2P/1B $ 85 - 110
Cottage, 2-4 Persons $ 150 - 190

XP $10-20. 2-6 pm check-in; 11 am check out. 2-night minimum stay on weekends; 3 or more nights required on holiday weekends. Deposit required; 2-week refund notice, 30-day notice for holidays; 30 days all year for cottages. Lower rates midweek.

2-story cedar-shake lodge surrounded by pines and oaks is decorated with country antiques; living room with fireplace, library and music alcove with piano. 9 guest rooms, each with private bath; 6 with fireplace. The self-contained cottage has a fireplace and whirlpool tub, breakfast not included. No pets. DS, MC, VI. Full breakfast served on the dining porch. No smoking.

❧ INDEPENDENCE

WILDER HOUSE
(760) 878-2119; FAX (760) 878-2320
325 Dusty Ln, 93526.

1P/1B $ 85 - 175   2P/1B $ 85 - 175

2 pm check-in; noon check out. Deposit required; 2-day refund notice. Lower rates in winter.

A contemporary home located on the Paiute Indian Reservation. 3 suites, 1 with private bath. Each room has TV, phone, air conditioning. Whirlpool; exercise/weight room. Horse and pet boarding available by advance request. DI, MC, VI. Full or continental breakfast. Box lunches, dinners available by advance request. Welcome basket in room upon arrival. Smoking on outside patio only.

WINNEDUMAH HOTEL, A BED & BREAKFAST INN   *(760) 878-2040;*
211 N Edwards St, 93526.   *FAX (760) 878-2040*

1P/1B $ 40 - 50   2P/2B $ 45 - 55

1 pm check-in; 11 am check out. Deposit required. Family rate.

A 1920s Western hotel has Spanish-American exterior and Craftsman interior, with many of the original furnishings. It once served as a retreat for Western-movie stars. 24 guest rooms, 17 with private bath. In-room air cooling. No pets. MC, VI. Continental breakfast served in the dining area. Smoking outside only.

❧ JOSHUA TREE

JOSHUA TREE INN
(760) 366-1188, (800) 366-1444;
61259 Twentynine Palms Hwy; Box 340, 92252.   *FAX (760) 366-3805*

1P/1B   ...   2P/1B $ 85 - 175   2P/2B $ 85 - 175

XP $10. Children ages 10 and under free. 2 pm check-in; noon check out. Deposit required; 3-day refund notice. Lower rates in summer.

A 1950s hacienda-style building with a mission tile roof sits in a desert location on the edge of town; rooms are positioned around the pool area. 7 guest rooms and 2 suites, each with private bath. Pool. Guest rooms air cooled. Pets allowed in some rooms, $10. AE, DI, DS, MC, VI. Full breakfast served in the dining room or on the patio. Refreshments served in the afternoon. Box lunches and dinners available by arrangement. Rooms for smokers and nonsmokers.

❦ JULIAN

THE ARTISTS' LOFT AND THE CABINS AT STRAWBERRY HILL
4811 Pine Ridge Ave; Box 2408, 92036.   *(760) 765-0765*

1P/1B $105 - 115   2P/1B $115 - 125
2P/1B Cabins $ 120 - 165

4-7 pm check-in; noon check out. 2-night minimum stay weekends. Deposit required; 7-day refund notice, 10% cancellation fee.

An active artists' studio on 5 acres has ocean and mountain views from the living and dining areas; garden teahouse and private picnic area. 2 guest rooms, each with private bath, CD player, books, art and wood-burning stove. The two cabins, on 3 and 6 acres respectively, are stocked with breakfast goods; 1 has a wood stove, 1 has a stone fireplace; both have CD players, dining and kitchen areas, and claw-foot tubs. No pets; resident cats. Full breakfast served from a menu in the courtyard or the dining/kitchen area. In-room coffee and tea. No smoking.

BUTTERFIELD B&B   *(760) 765-2179, (800) 379-4262;*
2284 Sunset Dr; Box 1115, 92036.   *FAX (760) 765-1229*

1P/1B $ 79 - 115   2P/1B $ 89 - 135

3 pm check-in; 11 am check out. 2-night minimum stay weekends and holidays. Deposit required; 7-day refund notice.

A country-style home with antique and country decor. Patio areas have a rock waterfall and gazebo. Rooms and cottage have fireplaces, featherbeds, in-room TV and country views. 4 guest rooms and cottage, each with private bath. Candlelit dinner and horse-drawn carriage available. DS, MC, VI. Gourmet breakfast served each morning. Smoking outside only.

EAGLENEST BED & BREAKFAST   *(760) 765-1252, (888) 345-6378*
2609 D St; Box 2513, 92036.

1P/1B $110 - 135   2P/1B $110 - 135

XP $20. 4 pm check-in; noon check out. 2-night minimum stay weekends and holidays. Deposit required; 7-day refund notice.

Victorian-style house set in historic district. 4 guest rooms, each with private bath. In-room TV and coffeemaker; 1 room with fireplace. Pool, whirlpool. DS, MC, VI. Full breakfast served in the dining area. Smoking outside only.

EDEN CREEK ORCHARD BED & BREAKFAST   *(760) 765-2102,*
1052 Julian Orchards Dr, 92036-0457.   *(800) 916-2739*

1P/1B $ 95 - 120   2P/1B $ 95 - 120   2P/2B $ 95 - 120

XP $20. 3 pm check-in; noon check out. 2-night minimum stay holidays and weekend nights that include Sat night. Credit card guarantee required; 7-day refund notice.

2 barn-style buildings with elegant country decor and antiques are situated in an apple orchard adjacent to a winery. 2 suites with private bath. In-room TV, fireplace, CD player, wet bar, refrigerator, coffeemaker. Hot tub, croquet, horseshoes, boccie ball. No pets. MC, VI. Continental breakfast served in the guest room, or voucher provided for full breakfast or lunch in town. In-room snacks. Smoking outside only.

HOMESTEAD BED & BREAKFAST   *(760) 765-1536*
4924 SR 79; Box 1208, 92036.

1P/1B $100 - 140   2P/1B $100 - 140   2P/2B $100 - 110

2 pm check-in; 11 am check out. 2-night minimum stay if Sat included. Deposit required; 7-day refund notice.

Contemporary 2-story mountain house features antiques and a stone fireplace. 4 guest rooms with private bath. No pets. MC, VI. Full breakfast served family style. Dessert and beverages served in the evening. Smoking outside only.

JULIAN GOLD RUSH HOTEL   *(760) 765-0201; reservations (800) 734-5854*
12032 Main St; Box 1856, 92036.

1P/1B $ 49   2P/1B $ 76 - 170   2P/2B $ 86 - 135

2 pm check-in; noon check out. 2-night minimum stay if Sat included. Deposit required; 2-day refund notice.

An 1897 Victorian hotel in the middle of the old gold-mining town contains period furnishings throughout and a wood-burning stove in lobby. 15 guest rooms with private bath; separate honeymoon cottage with fireplace. No pets. Full breakfast served in the dining area. Tea served in the afternoon. Smoking not permitted.

JULIAN WHITE HOUSE BED & BREAKFAST INN   *(760) 765-1764,*
3014 Blue Jay Dr; Box 824, 92036.   *(800) 948-4687; FAX (760) 765-1764*

1P/1B $ 90 - 145   2P/1B $ 90 - 145

4 pm check-in; noon check out. 2-night minimum stay weekends. Deposit required; 7-day refund notice; $25 cancellation fee.

Petite Southern mansion in a rural setting 4 miles from town. 3 guest rooms and 1 suite, each with private bath. Some rooms with gas fireplaces. Outdoor spa in rose garden. No pets. MC, VI. Full breakfast by candlelight. Evening dessert. Smoking outside only.

LEELIN'S WIKIUP BED & BREAKFAST   *(760) 765-1890, (800) 694-5487;*
1645 Whispering Pines Dr; Box 2363, 92036.   *FAX (760) 765-1512*

1P/1B   ...   2P/1B $125 - 150

3-5 pm check-in; noon check out. 2-night minimum stay required on weekends. Deposit required; 7-day refund notice. Midweek and weekend packages available.

Cedar and brick A-frame mountain lodge on 2½ acres of woods in Whispering Pines area has llamas and a donkey on premises. 7 guest rooms including 2 suites, each with private bath. 4 rooms have jetted baths or hot tubs, 4 rooms have fireplaces. Suites have refrigerator, microwave oven and coffeemaker. Large common room has fireplace and TV. Outdoor spa available for guests. Children's play area. Llama treks available. Small dogs allowed, $50 deposit; resident pets. MC, VI. Full breakfast Fri-Sun and expanded continental breakfast Mon-Thu, served in the dining room or on the deck (weather permitting). Afternoon snack provided; beverages and snacks available. Catered dinner available with advance notice; extra charge. Smoking outside in designated areas only.

MOUNTAIN HIGH BED & BREAKFAST   *(760) 765-1083*
4110 Deer Lake Park Rd; Box 268, 92036.

1P/1B   ...   2P/1B $125 - 140

2 pm check-in; noon check out. 2-night minimum stay weekends. Deposit required; 7-day refund notice. Discount on longer stays in cottage.

Wood-sided house and ivy-covered cottage are set amid tall pines on 3 acres of park-like grounds. Attached guest room with private entry, patio garden, bath, fireplace and TV; cottage has air conditioning, full kitchen, bath, wood-burning stove, deck, TV and VCR. Spa enclosed in gazebo. Hiking trails nearby. No pets. MC, VI. Full breakfast served in either the guest room or dining area. Refreshments served in the afternoon. Smoking outside only.

OAK HILL FARM

(760) 765-2356

3333 Coleman Cir; Box 2125, 92036.

| 1P/1B | $ 65 | 2P/1B | $ 75 |

XP $10. 2 pm check-in; 11 am check out. 2-night minimum stay weekends and holidays. Deposit required; 5-day refund notice. Lower rates Sun-Thu.

Colonial home and guest house feature period decor; buildings are surrounded by oak trees and are within walking distance of Julian's historic district. 2 guest rooms, each with private bath. In-room TV. Pool. No pets. AE, MC, VI. Continental breakfast served in the dining room. No smoking.

ORCHARD HILL COUNTRY INN

(760) 765-1700, (800) 716-7242

2502 Washington St; Box 425, 92036.

| 1P/1B | $140 - 195 | 2P/1B | $155 - 225 |

3-7 pm check-in; noon check out. 2-night minimum stay if including Fri or Sat. Deposit required; 7-day refund notice. Midweek discounts.

A 2-story lodge and 4 1928 California Craftsman cottages are located within the historic townsite. They feature American country decor, extensive gardens and porches. Lodge Great Room has a massive stone fireplace. 10 guest rooms in the lodge and 12 rooms in the cottages, each with private bath. In-room air conditioning, TV, VCRs; phone hookups available. Cottage rooms have fireplace, coffeemaker and bar; some have whirlpool. Hors d'oeuvres served in the afternoon. AE, MC, VI. Full breakfast served in the dining room, the patio or private porch. Smoking outside only.

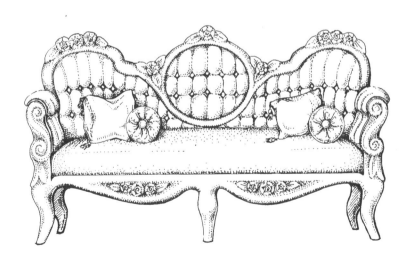

RANDOM OAKS RANCH BED & BREAKFAST COTTAGES   *(760) 765-1094,*
3742 Pine Hills Rd; Box 454, 92036.   *(800) 262-4344; FAX (760) 765-3979*

1P/1B $130 - 170   2P/1B $130 - 170

4 pm check-in; noon check out. Closed Thu. 2-night minimum stay if including Fri or Sat. Deposit required; 7-day refund notice. Champagne special Mon-Tue.

2 romantic private cottages are located on a Thoroughbred horse ranch. The English Squire Cottage features Queen Anne decor, a marble fireplace, half-canopy queen bed and a private deck with whirlpool. The Victorian Garden Cottage has a fireplace, Victorian cherry bed, and whirlpool accessed through French doors on private patio. Cottages have wet bars, small refrigerators and microwaves. MC, VI. Full breakfast served in cottages Fri-Wed. Complimentary in-room wine and snacks. Smoking outside only.

ROCKIN' A RANCH BED & BREAKFAST   *(760) 765-2820*
1531 Orchard Ln, 92036.

1P/1B   ...   2P/1B $125 - 160

3-5 pm check-in; noon check out. 2-night minimum stay weekends and holidays. Deposit required; 7-day refund notice.

Wood-sided country house sits on 5½ acres of orchards, with a stocked fishing pond and farm animals on premises. 3 guest rooms with private bath and fireplace, 1 with whirlpool tub for 2. Guests can pick fresh fruit in season and gather eggs. Pool; spa. No pets. MC, VI. Full breakfast. Pie served in the afternoon. Smoking outside only.

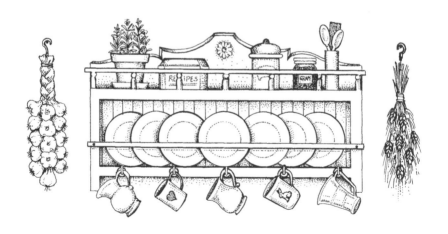

SEA STAR GUEST COTTAGE   *(760) 765-0502*
4041 Deer Lake Park Rd; Box 434, 92036.

1P/1B $125   2P/1B $125

2 pm check-in; 11 am check out. Deposit required.

A secluded romantic cottage set amid pine and oak trees 3 miles from town has a deck providing views of the surrounding mountains. Furnished with antiques, the cottage has a bedroom, bath, complete kitchen, fireplace, TV, barbecue and outdoor hot tub. Small pets allowed with prior approval. Continental breakfast served in the cottage.

SHADOW MOUNTAIN RANCH   *(760) 765-0323*
3 miles SW off SR 78/79 and Pine Hills Rd at 2771 Frisius Rd; Box 791, 92036.

1P/1B   ...   2P/1B $ 90 - 110

3 pm check-in; 11 am check out. 2-night minimum stay weekends. Deposit required; 7-day refund notice.

Ranch house with cottages and a tree house overlooks a meadow and pine-covered mountains. 6 guest rooms with private bath. In-room wood-burning stove and TV. Indoor lap pool; hot tub. No pets. Full breakfast served in the dining room or on the outdoor deck. Tea and snack served in the afternoon. Smoking outside only.

❦ KERNVILLE

KERN RIVER INN BED & BREAKFAST *(760) 376-6750, (800) 986-4382;*
119 Kern River Dr; Box 1725, 93238. *FAX (760) 376-6643*

1P/1B $ 79 - 89 2P/1B $ 89 - 99

XP $15. 3-6 pm check-in; 11 am check out. 2-night minimum stay weekends
Jun through Sep. Deposit required; 7-day refund notice. Winter rates Nov
through Mar (excluding holidays).

Victorian country inn has rooms individually decorated to capture the
character of the era; each room has a view of the Kern River. 6 rooms,
each with private bath. In-room air conditioning; phone available upon
request; most rooms have a fireplace or whirlpool. No pets. AE, MC, VI.
Full breakfast served in a separate dining area. Snacks served in the
afternoon. Smoking outside only.

WHISPERING PINES LODGE BED & BREAKFAST *(760) 376-3733,*
13745 Sierra Wy; Rte 1, Box 41, 93238. *(800) 241-4100; FAX (760) 376-3735*

1P/1B $ 99 - 119 Suite $129 - 159

XP $15. 3 pm check-in; 11 am check out. 2-night minimum stay weekends
May through Oct; 3 nights required on holiday weekends. Deposit required;
7-day refund notice; 30-day refund notice for holiday reservations.

Lodge and cottages overlook the Kern River and are furnished in a country
theme. 17 guest rooms, each with private bath. Balconies; 15 rooms with
fireplace; 5 rooms with kitchen; suite with whirlpool. In-room air
conditioning, refrigerator, phone, TV, VCR. Pool. No pets. AE, DI, MC, VI.
Full breakfast served in the lodge dining room or on the patio. Smoking
outside only.

❦ LAGUNA BEACH

THE CARRIAGE HOUSE
1322 Catalina St, 92651.

(949) 494-8945, (888) 335-8945;
FAX (949) 494-6829

1P/1B ...	2P/1B $ 95 - 150	2P/2B $125 - 150

XP $20. 2 pm check-in; 11 am check out. 2-night minimum stay weekends. Deposit required; 7-day refund notice; $10 cancellation fee.

Country-style Colonial inn filled with antiques is built around a central courtyard containing subtropical plants; located 2 blocks from the ocean. 6 guest suites, each with private bath, TV and VCR. Most suites have a fully equipped kitchen; some suites have 2 bedrooms. Pets allowed by prior arrangement. AE, MC, VI. Expanded continental breakfast served in the dining room or in the courtyard. Complimentary wine and fruit upon arrival. Smoking restricted.

CASA LAGUNA INN
2510 S Coast Hwy, 92651.

(949) 494-2996, (800) 233-0449;
FAX (949) 494-5009

1P/1B ...	2P/1B $ 79 - 249
Suites/Cottages $ 135 - 205	

XP $20. 2-9 pm check-in; 11 am check out. 2-night minimum stay Jul and Aug weekends and on holidays. Deposit required; 3-day refund notice.

Romantic inn with subtropical gardens, aviary and patios is set on a hillside overlooking the ocean. 21 guest accommodations, each with private bath. 1- and 2-bedroom suites with kitchen and dining room; 1- and 2-bedroom cottages with kitchen, dining room, living room and fireplace. In-room TV and direct-dial phones. Pool. Pets allowed by prior arrangement only. AE, DI, DS, MC, VI. Expanded continental breakfast served in the library or the garden. Tea, wine and hors d'oeuvres served in the afternoon. Rooms for smokers and nonsmokers.

EILER'S INN
741 S Coast Hwy, 92651.

(949) 494-3004

1P/1B $ 75 - 110	2P/1B $100 - 175	2P/2B $ 85 - 180

XP $20. 2 pm check-in; noon check out. Deposit required; 5-day refund notice; $10 cancellation fee.

A 1940s, 2-story New Orleans-style building centers around a courtyard with a fountain and many flowers. Located downtown, it is also close to the beach. 12 guest rooms, each with private bath. Classical guitar played on Sat. No pets. AE, MC, VI. Expanded continental breakfast served by the fireplace or on the patio. Wine, fruit and cheese served in the evening. Smoking outside only.

🍎 LA JOLLA

THE BED AND BREAKFAST INN AT LA JOLLA
7753 Draper Ave, 92037.
(858) 456-2066,
(800) 582-2466; FAX (858) 456-1510

1P/1B ...	2P/1B $110 - 250	2P/2B $120 - 180

3-5 pm check-in; 11 am check out. 2-night minimum stay weekends. Deposit required; 10-day refund notice.

A 1913 historical home in the San Diego Registry is filled with antiques. 15 rooms, each with private bath. Phone, air conditioning; some rooms with ocean view, fireplace, TV and mini bar. AE, MC, VI. Full gourmet breakfast served daily, and afternoon wine and cheese reception. In-room fresh flowers, sherry and fruit.

🍎 LAKE ARROWHEAD

BRACKEN FERN MANOR
(909) 337-8557; FAX (909) 337-3323
815 Arrowhead Villas Rd; Box 1006, 92352.

1P/1B ...	2P/1B $ 80 - 185	2P/2B $115

3:30 pm check-in; 11:30 am check out. 2-night minimum stay holidays. Deposit required; 3-day refund notice; 7-day refund notice on holidays.

This restored English Tudor-style manor built in 1929 was the community's first private membership resort hotel to have electricity. It is a historic landmark furnished with European antiques. 10 guest rooms, 8 with private bath, and family unit of 2 rooms with 1 shared bath. Bridal suite with whirlpool. Garden hot tub, indoor sauna, game parlor, art gallery/library, wine cellar and tasting, private garden patios and holiday events. No pets. MC, VI. Full breakfast served in the dining area. Afternoon tea, wine and cheese. Smoking outside only.

THE CARRIAGE HOUSE BED & BREAKFAST
(909) 336-1400,
(800) 526-5070
472 Emerald Dr; Box 982, 92352.

1P/1B $ 95 - 135	2P/1B $ 95 - 135

3 pm check-in; noon check out. 2-night minimum stay weekends, 3 nights required on some holidays. Deposit required; 7-day refund notice; $15 cancellation fee.

New England-style house hidden in the woods has views of Lake Arrowhead. Country decor is highlighted with feather beds and down comforters. 3 rooms, each with private bath; 1 with gas fireplace. Large sunroom and deck for gatherings; 2-person hammock. No pets. AE, DS, MC, VI. Full breakfast served in the dining area. Beverage and snacks offered in the afternoon. Smoking outside only.

CHATEAU DU LAC   *(909) 337-6488, (800) 601-8722; FAX (909) 337-6746*
3 miles N off SR 173 at 911 Hospital Rd; Box 1098, 92352.

1P/1B   ...   2P/1B $125 - 225

Noon-3 pm check-in; 11 am check out. 2-night minimum stay summer weekends. Deposit required; 3-day refund notice. Lower rates Sun-Thu.

Victorian house with French-country decor, many windows and lake views, built around a central atrium. 5 rooms, each with private bath. In-room TV, VCR and phone; some rooms have fireplace and whirlpool tub. Video library. No pets. AE, DS, MC, VI. Full breakfast served in the dining room. Afternoon tea at 4 pm. No smoking.

EAGLE'S LANDING   *(909) 336-2642, (800) 835-5085;*
27406 Cedarwood Dr; Box 1510, Blue Jay 92317.   *FAX (909) 336-2642*

1P/1B   ...   2P/1B $ 95 - 185   2P/2B $ 95 - 195

XP $15. 3 pm check-in; noon check out. 2-night minimum stay weekends, 2 or more nights required on holiday weekends. Deposit required; 7-day refund notice; $15 cancellation fee.

An elegant, mountain-style inn overlooking the lake is comfortably decorated with art, antiques and handicrafts, has a fireplace, and decks overlooking the lake. Located near Blue Jay. 4 guest rooms, each with private bath; 1 suite with TV, fireplace, bar and deck. No pets. AE, DS, MC, VI. Full breakfast served in the dining area. Beverages served in the evening. No smoking.

LITTLE BEAR BED & BREAKFAST   *(909) 337-5470, (888) 545-2327*
191 State Hwy 173, 92385.

1P/1B $ 80 - 100   2P/1B $ 80 - 120

3 pm check-in; 11 am check out. Deposit required; 7-day refund notice. Midweek rates.

A 2-story English Tudor-style house is just steps from the lake; village nearby. Two suites, each with private bath. Lake views, fireplace, antiques and cozy quilts. In-room cable TV. Children welcome. No pets. MC, VI. Full breakfast served in dining room. Little Bear cookies at bedtime. Complimentary wine and cheese upon arrival. Smoking outdoors only.

PROPHETS' PARADISE   *(909) 336-1969, (800) 987-2231*
26845 Modoc Ln; Box 2116, 92352.

1P/1B ...	2P/1B $ 90 - 160	2P/2B $125

XP $15. 4 pm check-in; noon check out. 2-night minimum stay weekends. Deposit required; 7-day refund notice; $15 cancellation fee.

Multilevel Tudor home in the mountains has leaded and stained glass windows and is furnished with antiques. 3 rooms, each with feather beds and private bath. Hot tub, fireplace and bar; billiard room, horseshoes and gym. In-room TV. Pets allowed. MC, VI. Full breakfast served in the guest room, dining room or on the deck. Hors d'oeuvres and beverages served Sat evening. Smoking outside only.

ROMANTIQUE LAKEVIEW LODGE   *(909) 337-6633, (800) 358-5253*
28051 Hwy 189; Box 128, 92352.

1P/1B $ 65 - 155	2P/1B $ 65 - 155	Suites $120 - 225

2-9 pm check-in; 11 am check out. 2-night minimum stay weekends Jul 1 through Jan 2 and on holidays. Deposit required; 7-day refund notice for weekends and holidays. Off-season rates.

A remodeled 1926 mountain lodge with romantic Victorian decor is located at the village. 9 rooms, each with private bath. In-room TV and VCR; most rooms have fireplace. No pets. AE, DS, MC, VI. Continental breakfast served in the dining area. Smoking outside only.

❦ LA QUINTA

TWO ANGELS INN   *(760) 564-7332, (888) 226-4546*
78-120 Caleo Bay Dr, 92253.

1P/1B $175 - 340	2P/1B $185 - 350	2P/2B $185 - 350

3 pm check-in; 11 am check out. 2-night minimum stay weekends and holidays Sep through May. Deposit required; 14-day refund notice. Lower rates Jun through Sep.

A French-style chateau has balconies, patios and old-world decor. 11 rooms with attached private bath, some with whirlpool tub. In-room air conditioning, TV, phone and fireplace. Piano, pool, hot tub available to guests. No pets. Facilities for retreats and small weddings. AE, DS, MC, VI. Full breakfast served in the dining room or on the terrace. Wine and hors d'oeuvres served in the afternoon. No smoking.

❦ LEMON COVE

MESA VERDE PLANTATION BED & BREAKFAST
33038 Sierra Hwy (SR 198), 93244.

(559) 597-2555,
(800) 240-1466

1P/1B $ 69 - 159   2P/1B $ 69 - 159

4 pm check-in; 11 am check out. Deposit required; 7-day refund notice.

Plantation-style country house not far from Sequoia National Park is surrounded by orange groves. Rooms are named after "Gone With the Wind" characters and decorated accordingly. 8 rooms, 6 with private bath. Some rooms with TV, VCR, fireplace, whirlpool bath and veranda. Heated pool, spa and gazebos. No pets. AE, DI, DS, MC, VI. Full gourmet vegetarian breakfast served in the dining room or courtyard. No smoking.

❦ LONG BEACH

KENNEBEC CORNER INN
2305 E 2nd St, 90803.

(562) 439-2705

Sun-Thu	1P/1B	$ 85	2P/1B	$ 95
Fri-Sat	1P/1B	$ 125	2P/1B	$140

4 pm check-in; noon check out. Closed Dec 24-25. Reservations required. Deposit required; 7-day refund notice.

The 2-story California Craftsman house, built in 1923, is located in the Bluff Park historic district. 1 3-room suite with private bath. Private phone and fax, cable TV, fireplace, mini-fridge. Sitting room with fireplace, and courtyard with whirlpool. No pets. MC, VI. Expanded continental breakfast Mon-Fri, full breakfast Sat-Sun, served on the patio or in a separate dining room. Complimentary beverages. Smoking on private balcony or courtyard patio only.

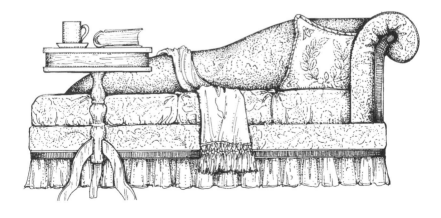

❦ LOS ANGELES

THE INN AT 657
657 W 23rd St, 90007.   *(213) 741-2200, (800) 347-7512*

1P/1B $ 75 - 95   2P/1B $110   2P/2B $150

XP $15. 2 pm check-in; 11 am check out. Deposit required; 5-day refund notice.

2-story, renovated neoclassical inn with garden patios is near the University of Southern California and the Los Angeles Convention Center. 4 suites with living room, kitchen and bath (2 have 1 bedroom, 1 has 2 bedrooms, 1 has 3 bedrooms and 2 baths). Suites have in-room phone, cable TV and air conditioning. No pets. Full breakfast served in the dining room. Smoking outside only.

RAINBOW'S END BED & BREAKFAST   *(323) 650-2345*
1618 Mountcrest Ave, 90069.

1P/1B $110 - 175   2P/1B $110 - 175

XP $20. Noon check-in; 11 am check out. Deposit required; 7-day refund notice; $20 cancellation fee.

Located high in the Hollywood Hills above Sunset Boulevard, this modern residence, built in 1990, offers sweeping views of the Los Angeles Basin on a clear day. 2 bedrooms, each with private bath, can accommodate 2 couples or a family of up to 5. In-room phone, TV, air conditioning. No pets. Continental or full breakfast served in the dining room. Afternoon or evening cakes and beverages. Smoking outside only.

❦ MAMMOTH LAKES

CINNAMON BEAR INN BED & BREAKFAST
113 Center St, 93546.

(760) 934-2873,
(800) 845-2873; FAX (760) 934-2873

1P/1B	$ 59 - 84	2P/1B	$ 69 - 114	2P/2B	$ 89 - 139

XP $10. 3 pm check-in; 10 am check out. Deposit required; 7-day refund notice. Ski packages and off-season (summer) rates.

This New England-style lodge has guest rooms in an adjacent building. 22 rooms, each with private bath; some rooms have 4-poster beds. In-room phones, TV. Some rooms have kitchens, some have fireplaces. Whirlpool available. AE, DS, MC, VI. Full breakfast served in the lodge. Afternoon refreshments. Smoking outside only.

KATHERINE'S HOUSE
201 Waterford Ave, 93546.

(760) 934-2991, (800) 934-2991;
FAX (760) 924-5903

1P/1B	$ 85 - 140	2P/1B	$ 85 - 140

Cabin, 2-4 Persons $ 130 - 245

XP $20-25. 4 pm check-in; 11 am check out. 2-night minimum stay holidays. Deposit required; 7-day refund notice. Lower rates in summer.

Contemporary chalet home with original artwork. Located in a residential neighborhood among pine and aspen trees. Chalet has 2 rooms, 1 with private bath. Morning suite has fireplace and whirlpool tub for 2. Cabin has wood burner. Gourmet kitchen for guests' use. In-room phone, TV, VCR. Dogs welcome; one resident dog. MC, VI. Coffee/tea served in guest room. Expanded continental breakfast available in serving area. Afternoon wine and appetizers. No smoking.

MAMMOTH COUNTRY INN
75 Joaquin Rd, 93546.

(760) 934-2710, (800) 358-2710;
FAX (760) 924-5827

1P/1B	$ 69 - 85	2P/1B	$ 79 - 95

XP $15. 4 pm check-in; 10 am check out. 2-night minimum stay weekends. Deposit required. Lower rates in summer and spring.

A newly decorated 1950s lodge-style house is tucked away in the woods near the shopping district. Each room is decorated with a different theme. 7 guest rooms, 1 with private bath. In-room TV, VCR. Large lounge with stone fireplace. Fully equipped kitchen for guests' use. No pets. AE, DS, MC, VI. Full breakfast. Smoking outside only.

🍂 MORRO BAY

MARINA STREET INN *(805) 772-4016, (888) 683-9389;*
305 Marina St, 93442. *FAX (805) 772-0667*

1P/1B $ 89 - 140   2P/1B $ 89 - 140

1 pm check-in; 11 am check out. 3-day cancellation notice.

Cape Cod style inn. 4 mini-suites, each with private bath. AE, MC, VI. Full breakfast served in the dining room or courtyard. Complimentary wine and cheese served at 5:30 pm. No smoking.

SNOW GOOSE INN *(805) 934-2660, (800) 874-7368*
57 Forest Tr.; Box 387, 93546.

2P/1B $ 58 - 98   2P/2B $ 58 - 168

XP $6-12. 2 pm check-in; 10 am check out. 2-night minimum stay holidays and weekends in winter. Deposit required; 30-day refund notice in winter. Off-season (summer) rates.

Contemporary 2-story country inn is located within walking distance of shops and restaurants in town. 15 rooms, each with private bath; 4 2-bedroom apartments; 2 kitchen units. Outdoor hot tub. In-room TV and phone. TV and VCR in the common room. No pets. DI, DS, MC, VI. Full breakfast served in the dining area. Appetizers served in the evening. No smoking.

❧ NEWPORT BEACH

DORYMAN'S OCEANFRONT INN *(949) 675-7300, (800) 634-3303;*
2102 W Ocean Front, 92663. *FAX (949) 675-7300*
1P/1B ... 2P/1B $135 - 275

XP $25. 4 pm check-in; noon check out. Deposit required; 3-day refund notice; cancellation fee.

Oceanfront 2-floor inn with Victorian furnishings, patio and rooftop sun deck is located near the Pacific Ocean. 10 guest rooms, each with private bath; 2 2-room suites. Up to 4 persons accommodated in suites with 2 beds. Most rooms have ocean view. Fireplace in each guest room; ocean view and whirlpool in some rooms. No pets. AE, MC, VI. Expanded continental breakfast served in the parlor, on the patio or in guest rooms. Smoking in designated areas.

PORTOFINO BEACH HOTEL *(949) 673-7030, (800) 571-8749;*
2306 W Ocean Front, 92663. *FAX (949) 723-4370*
1P/1B $129 - 379 2P/1B $129 - 379 2P/2B $129 - 379

3 pm check-in; noon check out. 3-day refund notice.

European-style inn near the Newport Pier overlooks the ocean. 15 rooms and 5 furnished apartments, each with private bath. In-room air conditioning, phone and TV; most rooms have whirlpool, ocean view and fireplace. No pets. AE, CB, DI, MC, VI. Expanded continental breakfast served in the fireplace lounge area. Room service available from adjacent restaurant.

❧ NIPOMO

THE KALEIDOSCOPE INN *(805) 929-5444*
130 E Dana St; Box 1297, 93444.
1P/1B ... 2P/1B $ 90

XP $10. 3-8 pm check-in; noon check out. 2-night minimum stay holiday weekends. Deposit required; 24-hour refund notice; $10 cancellation fee if room is not re-rented.

An 1887 Victorian house with framed stained glass windows is furnished with antiques and sits in an acre of gardens with a gazebo. 3 guest rooms, each with private bath, 1 with a whirlpool tub. No pets. AE, MC, VI. Full breakfast served in the dining room or the gardens. Smoking outside only.

❦ NIPTON

HOTEL NIPTON
(760) 856-2335

72 Nipton Rd; HCR #1, Box 357, 92364.

1P/1B ...	2P/1B $ 55	2P/2B $ 55

XP $10. Noon check-in; 11 am check out. Deposit required; 2-day refund notice; 10% cancellation fee.

Early 1900s, renovated adobe hotel is located in the Mojave National Preserve. 4 guest rooms with 2 shared baths. Hotel contains central air conditioning and two outdoor whirlpools. No pets. DS, MC, VI. Continental breakfast served in the hotel parlor. Smoking outside only.

❦ OJAI

THEODORE WOOLSEY HOUSE
(805) 646-9779

1484 E Ojai Ave, 93023.

1P/1B ...	2P/1B $ 95 - 150

XP $20. 2 pm check-in; noon check out. 2-night minimum stay with Sat night. 5-day refund notice. Midweek rates.

An 1887, 2-story, stone-and-clapboard New England farmhouse lies among 7 acres of oak trees, 1 mile east of town in Ojai's Shangri-La. The house has 2 fireplaces, a screened-in patio and a garden room. 5 guest rooms, 1 cottage; each with private bath. Air conditioning; 4 rooms with TV and phone; 2 rooms with fireplace; 3 rooms with balcony; 1 room with sun deck. Cottage has fireplace. Pool, hot tub. No pets. Expanded continental breakfast served buffet-style in the dining room. Refreshments served in the afternoon. Smoking outside only.

❦ PALM DESERT

TRES PALMAS BED AND BREAKFAST   *(760) 773-9858, (800) 770-9858*
73-135 Tumbleweed Ln, 92260.

1P/1B $110 - 175   2P/1B $110 - 175

XP $20. 3-8 pm check-in; 11 am check out. 2-night minimum stay weekends. Deposit required; 7-day refund notice. Special rates Jun 15 through Oct 15.

A 1-story home decorated in Southwest style is located 1 block from El Paseo-area shopping, galleries and restaurants. 4 rooms, each with private bath. In-room air conditioning, ceiling fan and cable TV. Pool, whirlpool. No pets. AE, MC, VI. Expanded continental breakfast can be eaten in the dining room or by the pool, or guests may take a tray to their room. Iced tea and lemonade served all day; afternoon snacks. Smoking not permitted.

❦ PALM SPRINGS

KORAKIA PENSIONE   *(760) 864-6411*
257 S Patencio Rd, 92262.

1P/1B   ...   2P/1B $109 - 365

XP $38. 3 pm check-in; noon check out. Closed mid-Jul through the day before Labor Day. 2-night minimum stay weekends. Deposit required; 14-day refund notice. Lower rates Jul 5-31.

Restored 1920s Moroccan villa at the foot of Mt. San Jacinto is 4 blocks from downtown Palm Springs; rooms are furnished with antiques. Winston Churchill was once a guest at this home. 20 guest rooms/suites, each with private bath. Expanded continental breakfast served in the guest room or on the patio; full breakfast on Sun. Moroccan tea served on weekend afternoons. In-room air conditioning, phone and refrigerator; some rooms have fireplace and kitchen. 2 pools; hiking trails nearby. No pets. Smoking outside only.

THE WILLOWS HISTORIC PALM SPRINGS INN   *(760) 320-0771,*
412 W Tahquitz Canyon Wy, 92262.   *(800) 966-9597; FAX (760) 320-0780*

1P/1B $175 - 500   2P/1B $175 - 500

4 pm check-in; noon check out. 2-night minimum stay holidays and weekends. Full payment required at time of reservation; 7-day refund notice. Summer rates.

A restored, 1927 historic Mediterranean-style villa is set against the mountains just west of downtown. Original stone path through hillside garden; mountain waterfall just outside dining room. 8 guest rooms, each with private bath, stone fireplace, cable TV, telephone and data port. No pets. AE, CB, DI, DS, MC, VI. Full gourmet breakfast. Afternoon hors d'oeuvres. No smoking.

❦ PASADENA

PASADENA HOTEL BED & BREAKFAST   *(626) 568-8172, (800) 653-8886;*
76 N Fair Oaks Ave, 91103.   *FAX (626) 793-6409*

1P/1B $ 65 - 115   2P/1B $ 75 - 135

XP $10. Parking $5 in adjacent lot. 2 pm check-in; noon check out. 2-night minimum stay over New Year's. Deposit required; 2-day refund notice.

Restored historic hotel with early-European furnishings and courtyard is located in Old Pasadena. 12 rooms have 5 shared baths. In-room TV and phone. No pets. AE, MC, VI. Expanded continental breakfast served in breakfast nook. Smoking outside only.

❦ PASO ROBLES

ARBOR INN BED & BREAKFAST   *(805) 227-4673; FAX (805) 227-1112*
2130 Arbor Rd; Box 3260, 93447.

1P/1B   ...   2P/1B $115 - 235

3 pm check-in; 11 am check out. Deposit required; 7-day refund notice.

Neo-Victorian inn is located in a vineyard across from Treana Winery. 8 rooms and penthouse suite, each with private bath, fireplace and balcony with vineyard view. Full breakfast served in dining room. Beverage and hors d'oeuvres served in afternoon. In-room air conditioning. No pets. MC, VI. Smoking outside only.

THE JUST INN   *(805) 237-4150, (800) 726-0049*
11680 Chimney Rock Rd, 93446.

1P/1B $225 - 275   2P/1B $225 - 275

3 pm check-in; noon check out. 2-night minimum stay weekends. Deposit required; 10-day refund notice. Seasonal midweek rates.

2-story French Provincial winery is surrounded by rolling hills and acres of vineyards. 3 suites, each with private bath. Individual rooms are decorated for a different area in Europe (Provence, Tuscany and Sussex), with in-room fireplace, phone and air conditioning. Pool, whirlpool and hot tub; mountain bikes available for guests' use. Pets not allowed in guest room. AE, DS, MC, VI. Full breakfast served in the guest room or dining area. Justin Wines, cheese and fruit platter, and picnic lunches available; additional charge. Dinner available nightly in Deborah's Room; additional charge. Guest Chef Candlelight Dinners are scheduled throughout the year. Smoking outside only.

THE WILD ROSE INN BED & BREAKFAST   *(805) 239-2331,*
250 Wild Rose Ln, 93446.   *(888) 909-2331; FAX (805) 239-7940*

1P/1B $ 85 - 145   2P/1B $ 85 - 145

XP $65. 3 pm check-in; 11 am check out. 2-night minimum stay holidays. Deposit required; 7-day refund notice. Midweek and corporate rates.

Two story house with brick and wood siding is set in a 20-acre almond ranch. The house has a 360-degree view of orchards, vineyards and rolling hills. Interior has English country decor with antiques. 2 suites and 1 guest room, each with private bath, TV, radio, refrigerator, microwave, in-room coffee and hair dryer. 1 suite has fireplace; both suites have spa tub. No pets. DI, DS, MC, VI. Expanded continental breakfast weekdays; full gourmet breakfast weekends. Smoking outside only.

❦ PLAYA DEL REY

INN AT PLAYA DEL REY   *(310) 574-1920; FAX (310) 574-9920*
435 Culver Blvd, 90293.

1P/1B $125 - 275   2P/1B $125 - 275   2P/2B $125 - 275

XP $15. 3 pm check-in; noon check out. Deposit required; 3-day refund notice.

Contemporary New England-style inn has spacious rooms, many facing Marina del Rey and the Ballona wetlands. 22 guest rooms, each with private bath. In-room air conditioning, TV, phone and data port; 13 rooms with whirlpool tub. Whirlpool in common area; bicycles. No pets. AE, MC, VI. Full breakfast served in dining room. Tea, wine and cheese served every afternoon. No smoking. All rooms wheelchair accessible.

❦ PONDEROSA

MOUNTAIN TOP BED & BREAKFAST   *(559) 542-2639; FAX (559) 542-1318*
56816 Aspen Dr, Springville 93265.

1P/1B $ 70   2P/1B $ 80   2P/2B $ 80

XP $10. 2 pm check-in; 11 am check out. 7-day refund notice; $10 processing fee applied to all cancellations.

This remodeled wood-frame mountain house, located in Sequoia National Forest, has a large stone fireplace. 2 guest rooms with shared bath. In-room VCR with complimentary movies. Spa room. No pets; resident dog. AE, MC, VI. Hot gourmet breakfast served in dining area. Wine and cheese served later in the day. Smoking permitted on outside deck only.

❦ POSEY

PANORAMA HEIGHTS BED AND BREAKFAST
45758 Guhl Ave, 93260.

(805/661) 536-8971;
FAX (805) 536-8738

1P/1B $ 85	2P/1B $ 85	2P/2B $ 85

XP $10. 3 pm check-in; 11 am check out. Deposit required; 2-day refund notice. Midweek and multiday rates.

Located northeast of Bakersfield and southeast of Porterville, in the Sequoia National Forest, is a mountain lodge built in 1948. The 2-story home sits on an acre of landscaped grounds. 3 guest rooms, each with private bath. Living room has fireplace, TV, VCR and stereo. Reading area and guest refrigerator located on second floor. Fax and phone available. Pets allowed; resident pets include 2 dogs, 1 cat, and 1 parrot. Full breakfast served in separate serving area. Evening snacks provided; other meals available. Smoking outside only.

ROAD'S END AT POSO CREEK
Rural Rte 1; Box 450, 93260.

(805/661) 536-8668

Per person $75

3 pm check-in; 1 pm check out. 2-night minimum stay weekends. Deposit required; 14-day refund notice; $10 cancellation fee. Weekly rates.

A 1920s restored mountain home with fireplace, wood stove and loft sits beside a creek in Sequoia National Forest. Accommodates 1 guest party at a time; 1 bedroom with private deck and bath; loft bedroom with half bath. TV in main room. Treetop deck. Hiking, fishing and cross-country skiing nearby. Chains may be required Dec through May. No pets; resident cat. Full breakfast served in the dining area, the garden or forest. Lunch and dinner can be catered by prior arrangement; additional charge. Smoking outside only.

❦ Rancho Cucamonga

CHRISTMAS HOUSE BED AND BREAKFAST INN *(909) 980-6450*
9240 Archibald Ave, 91730.

1P/1B   ...   2P/1B $ 80 - 180

4-7 pm check-in; 11 am check out. Deposit required; 7-day refund notice.

A 1904, Queen Anne Victorian house is 3 stories and features red-and-green stained glass, intricate wood carvings, antique furnishings and landscaped gardens. 6 guest rooms, 4 with private bath; 1 2-room suite with 2 fireplaces; 2 suites with private courtyard and covered whirlpool; 1 room with fireplace and whirlpool. TV available by request; air conditioning. Fireplace in some rooms. No pets. AE, DS, MC, VI. Full breakfast served in the dining room or guest rooms. Smoking outside only.

❦ Randsburg

THE COTTAGE HOTEL BED AND BREAKFAST *(760) 374-2285,*
130 Butte Ave; Box D, 93554.   *(888) 268-4622; FAX (760) 374-2132*

1P/1B $ 65 - 75   2P/1B $ 75 - 85
2P/2B (Cottage) $ 75 - 85

XP $10. 4-7 pm check-in; noon check out. Deposit required; 2-day refund notice. Midweek rates.

A restored wood-and-stucco hotel from the early 1900s is located in a historic gold-mining town. The inn has Victorian furnishings, local artifacts, ample common areas and gardens. 4 guest rooms, each with private bath and ceiling fan, plus a housekeeping cottage. Refrigerator and microwave available. Antique and gift shop. No pets. AE, DI, MC, VI. Expanded continental breakfast served in the dining room. Teas, juices and hors d'oeuvres served at sundown. Smoking outside only.

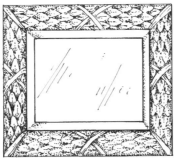

❧ RED MOUNTAIN

OLD OWL INN BED & BREAKFAST & COTTAGES   *(760) 374-2235,*
701 US 395, 93558.   *(888) 653-6954; FAX (760) 374-2354*

1P/1B	$ 45 - 55	2P/1B	$ 45 - 55	2P/2B	$ 45 - 65

XP $10. 2 pm check-in; 11 am check out. Deposit required; 2-day refund notice.

Historic gambling hall with bar and some furnishings from the 1920s is located in the Rand mining district of the Mojave Desert. 2 cottages with private bath. Air conditioning, TV, kitchen and snack basket. Pets allowed. DS, MC, VI. Large continental breakfast served in cottages. Sandwiches and dessert available midday or evening; extra charge. Smoking outside only.

❧ RIDGECREST

BEVLEN HAUS BED & BREAKFAST   *(760) 375-1988, (800) 375-1989*
809 N Sanders St, 93555.

1P/1B	$ 45	2P/1B	$ 55 - 65

3 pm check-in; 11 am check out. Deposit required; 1-day refund notice.

Rambling ranch house located near town center has antique kitchen fixtures and sitting-room furnishings. 3 guest rooms, each with private bath. In-room air cooling. Whirlpool. AE, DS, MC, VI. Full breakfast is served in the dining room. Alcoholic beverages not permitted in rooms. No smoking.

❧ RUNNING SPRINGS

SPRING OAKS BED & BREAKFAST INN AND MOUNTAIN RETREAT
CENTER   *(909) 867-7797, (800) 867-9636*
2465 Spring Oak Dr; Box 2918, 92382.

1P/1B	$ 85 - 130	2P/1B	$ 95 - 130

3-6 pm check-in; noon check out. Deposit required; 3-day refund notice.

Wood-sided house with large fireplace, knotty pine interior and country decor overlooks the valley. 3 guest rooms, 1 with private bath. Hot tub; massage therapy available. Hiking tours to hot springs and to other inns in the region are available. Monthly concerts. Ski packages. No pets. MC, VI. Full breakfast served in a separate dining area. Wine and cheese served 4-5 pm. No smoking.

❦ SAN CLEMENTE

CASA TROPICANA BED & BREAKFAST INN   *(949) 492-1234;*
610 Avenida Victoria, 92672.   *FAX (949) 492-2423*

1P/1B   ...   2P/1B $ 85 - 350

XP $15. 3:30 pm check-in; 11:30 am check out. 2-night minimum stay weekends and some holidays. Deposit required; 10-day refund notice; fee. Midweek rates.

A 1992 Spanish-style home near the pier overlooks the ocean. Each room is individually decorated with a tropical island theme. 9 guest rooms, each with private bath; 7 with whirlpool tub; 8 with fireplaces; 5 with ocean view. Penthouse has private 5th-floor deck with outdoor hot tub. In-room cable TV, radio, phone. No pets. AE, MC, VI. Two full breakfast entrees served on the patio. No smoking.

❦ SAN DIEGO

ASIA EDEN BED AND BREAKFAST   *(619) 544-6045; FAX (619) 239-5577*
1610 Union St, 92101.

1P/1B $ 95 - 105   2P/1B $100 - 125   2P/2B $115 - 150

XP $15. 1 pm check-in; noon check out. 2-night minimum stay weekends and holidays. Deposit required; 10-day refund notice. Discount for seniors and longer stays.

Two restored Victorian homes, circa 1890s, with modern amenities. Centrally located near San Diego attractions. 8 guest rooms decorated with oriental antiques and furnishings, each with private bath; 4 with full kitchen; 2 with fireplace; all with air conditioning. In-room phone, cable TV. Children welcome, baby room available. No pets. AE, DS, MC, VI. Full breakfast served in dining room. Smoking outside on the front porch only.

BEACH AREA HOUSE BED & BREAKFAST/ELSBREE HOUSE CONDO
(619) 226-4133, (800) 510-6975; FAX (619) 223-4133
5054 Narragansett Ave, 92107.

1P/1B $ 85 - 95   2P/1B $ 95 - 105

4 pm check-in; 11 am check out. 2-night minimum stay weekends and holidays. Deposit required; 10-day refund notice; $25 cancellation fee. Separate 3-bedroom, 3-bath condo with kitchen sleeps 6; $250 per night/ 4-night minimum stay or $1250 per week.

Contemporary Cape Cod-style home in the Ocean Beach area is located ½ block from the beach in a residential area. Decorated with wicker, oak and Country English floral prints, it features many private patios and balconies. 5 guest rooms, each with private bath and private entrance. No pets. AE, MC, VI. Expanded continental breakfast served in the dining room. Smoking outside only.

BEARS AT THE BEACH BED & BREAKFAST   *(858) 272-2578*
1047 Grand Ave, 92109.

1P/1B $ 92 - 116   2P/1B $ 92 - 116

XP $20. 2-6 pm check-in; noon check out. 3-night minimum stay weekends and holidays. Weekly rates also available. Deposit required; 10-day refund notice.

Built in 1952 in the Pacific Beach district, the house is near both Mission Bay and the Pacific Ocean. Amenities include in-room cable TV, ceiling fan, stereo tape deck, beach towels, a private walled garden patio and a collection of stuffed bears. Fully equipped kitchen. 2 rooms, 1 with private bath. No pets. MC, VI. Continental breakfast; homemade cookies. Smoking outside only.

BLOM HOUSE BED & BREAKFAST   *(858) 467-0890, (800) 797-2566*
1372 Minden Dr, 92111.

1P/1B $ 79   2P/1B $ 85 - 95
2-Bedroom/bath wing $ 120 for 4 persons, $ 95 for 1 or 2 persons.

XP $15. Noon check-in; 11 am check out. 2-night minimum stay weekends. Deposit required; 10-day refund notice. Midweek, weekly and senior rates.

Cottage-style home with high ceilings, hardwood floors and antique furnishings is in a residential neighborhood overlooking Hotel Circle and Fashion Valley Mall. 2 guest rooms, each with private bath; 1 2-bedroom suite with bath. In-room air conditioning, phone, TV, VCR and refrigerator with snacks. Hot tub on deck. Video library. Small pets allowed. AE, CB, DI, DS, JCB, MC, VI. Full breakfast served in a separate dining area. Smoking outside only.

CAROLE'S BED & BREAKFAST INN   *(619) 280-5258, (800) 975-5521*
3227 Grim Ave, 92104.

1P/1B	$ 59 - 79	2P/1B	$ 69 - 89	2P/2B	$ 69 - 89

XP $10. Noon check-in; 11 am check out. 2-night minimum stay on weekends. Deposit required; 10-day refund notice.

Historic 2-story bungalow built in 1904 by the city's mayor is furnished with antiques and a piano; a rose garden is on the grounds. Located 1½ miles east of Balboa Park and the San Diego Zoo. 4 guest rooms; 1 with private bath, 3 with shared baths. In-room TV. Pool, hot tub and gas barbecue. No pets. AE, DS, MC, VI. Full breakfast served in the guest room or dining area. Afternoon refreshments. Dinner available upon request; additional charge. Smoking outside only.

THE COTTAGE   *(619) 299-1564*
3829 Albatross St; Box 3292, 92163.

1P/1B	$ 65 - 95	2P/1B	$ 59 - 95

XP $10. 4 pm check-in; noon check out. 2-night minimum stay required. Deposit required; 7-day refund notice.

A 1913, homestead-style redwood cottage and a house featuring Victorian furnishings are located in the Hillcrest section of old homes. The cottage guest suite has a private bath and contains a wood-burning stove, kitchen and a pump organ; in the main house 1 guest room with private bath has a separate entrance. In-room TV, phone and refrigerator. No pets. AE, MC, VI. Continental breakfast served in the dining area. No smoking.

HARBOR HILL GUEST HOUSE   *(619) 233-0638*
2330 Albatross St, 92101.

1P/1B	...	2P/1B	$ 65 - 95	2P/2B	$ 65 - 95

XP $10. 1 pm check-in; 11 am check out. 2-night minimum stay weekends. 3-day refund notice. Special rates for longer stays.

A 1920s 3-level house and adjacent carriage house have traditional furnishings with sun deck and garden that overlook San Diego Harbor. 6 guest rooms, each with private bath; carriage house with kitchen and private balcony. Some rooms with harbor view. Use of kitchen on each level. In-room phone and TV. No pets. MC, VI. No-host continental breakfast.

HERITAGE PARK BED AND BREAKFAST INN
(619) 299-6832,
2470 Heritage Park Row, 92110.   *(800) 995-2470; FAX (619) 299-9465*

| 1P/1B | $ 85 - 150 | 2P/1B | $ 90 - 200 | 2P/2B | $ 90 - 200 |
| Suite | $225 - 265 |

3 pm check-in; 11 am check out. 2-night minimum stay weekends. Deposit required; 7-day refund notice.

An 1889, 2-story Queen Anne-style mansion contains antique furnishings, and has a spacious veranda and a corner tower. It is located in historic Old Town near other Victorian structures. 10 guest rooms, each with private bath; 2-bedroom suite with whirlpool tub. In-room phones. Film classics shown nightly. No pets. DI, DS, MC, VI. Full breakfast served in the dining room. Afternoon tea served in the parlor and in the garden. Candlelit dinners by special request; extra charge. Smoking outside only.

KEATING HOUSE
(619) 239-8585, (800) 995-8644;
2331 2nd Ave, 92101-1505.   *FAX (619) 239-5774*

| 1P/1B | $ 70 - 95 | 2P/1B | $ 70 - 95 |

XP $30. Check-in by appointment; noon check out. 2-night minimum stay holidays. Deposit required; 7-day refund notice.

An 1888, Queen Anne Victorian house with an octagonal turret, a veranda, stained glass, and antique furnishings sits above San Diego Bay near Balboa Park. 8 rooms, 2 with private bath. No pets. AE, DS, MC, VI. Full breakfast served in the dining room. Smoking outside only.

VILLA SERENA BED & BREAKFAST INN
(619) 224-1451, (800) 309-2778
2164 Rosecrans St, 92106.

| 1P/1B | $ 85 - 95 | 2P/1B | $ 85 - 95 | 2P/2B | $ 85 - 95 |

XP $25. Entire house available for $220 per day. 3 pm check-in; noon check out. 2-night minimum stay weekends and holidays. Credit card guarantee; 7-day refund notice; up to $95 cancellation fee. Weekly and off-season (Sep through Dec) rates.

2-story, Mediterranean-style Italian villa built around a courtyard and located close to beaches and tourist attractions, with SeaWorld and Old Town just 5 minutes away. 2 upstairs bedrooms and downstairs suite each have private bath. Bedrooms can be converted into a family suite. Suite has fireplace, queen bed, view and door to garden and pool/spa. No pets. DS, MC, VI. Full breakfast served in dining room or garden. Snacks and beverages available to guests. Guests have access to refrigerator and may bring drinks or food. Smoking outside only.

🍎 SAN LUIS OBISPO

GARDEN STREET INN   *(805) 545-9802, (800) 488-2045; FAX (805) 781-7469*
1212 Garden St, 93401.

1P/1B ...   2P/1B $ 90 - 120   Suites $140 - 160
3-7 pm check-in; 11 am check out. 2-night minimum stay holidays and some weekends. Deposit required; 7-day refund notice.

An 1887, Italian-style Queen Anne house, adorned with stained glass windows as well as a dramatic staircase and antique furnishings, is located in the heart of downtown San Luis Obispo. 9 guest rooms and 4 suites, each with private bath. In-room air conditioning and radio; 5 rooms with gas fireplace; 6 rooms with whirlpool tub. No pets. AE, MC, VI. Full breakfast served in the dining area or suite. Wine and cheese served in the afternoon. Smoking outside only.

HERITAGE INN   *(805) 544-7440*
978 Olive St, 93405.

1P/1B $ 60 - 120   2P/1B $ 85 - 130

XP $10. 3-8 pm check-in; 11 am check out. 2-night minimum stay holiday weekends and on weekends Jun through Oct. Deposit required; 7-day refund notice.

A 3000-square-foot Victorian Craftsman inn nestled near a creekside garden has mountain views from the balconies. Built circa 1900 by the constable, Manuel Herrera, it is within walking distance of quaint downtown and minutes from sightseeing and beaches. 7 guest rooms, 3 with private bath; 4 with in-room sink and 2 shared baths. Each room is unique with either fireplace, window seat or walk-out terrace and all are furnished with antiques. Pets allowed by prior arrangement; resident cat. AE, MC, VI. Full breakfast is served in the fireside dining room. Wine and cheese served later in the day. Smoking outside only.

❦ SANTA BARBARA

THE BATH STREET INN
(805) 682-9680, (800) 341-2284;
1720 Bath St, 93101.
FAX (805) 569-1281

1P/1B $ 80 - 200   2P/1B $ 85 - 205

2 pm check-in; 11 am check out. 2-night minimum stay if including Sat. Deposit required; 3-day refund notice.

An 1890, 3-story Queen Anne Victorian house with a semicircular balcony, antique furnishings, patio and courtyards is located a few blocks from downtown. 12 guest rooms, each with private bath; 3 rooms with whirlpool and fireplace; 2 rooms with whirlpool, 1 with fireplace. In-room TV and phone; some with VCR. Library. No pets. AE, MC, VI. Full gourmet breakfast served in the dining room or in the garden. Tea served in the afternoon, refreshments served in the evening. Smoking outside only.

BLUE DOLPHIN INN
(805) 965-2333; FAX (805) 962-9470
420 W Montecito St, 93101.

1P/1B $ 98 - 195   2P/1B $ 98 - 195   2P/2B $115 - 195

XP $15. 3 pm check-in; noon check out. 2-night minimum stay weekends and holidays. Deposit required; 7-day refund notice. Weekly and off-season rates.

This Victorian house with antique furnishings is located close to the beach and the wharf. 9 rooms with private bath; some have fireplace, 3 have whirlpool. 3 suites, including a honeymoon suite. DI, MC, VI. Full breakfast served in dining room. Wine and cheese served in the afternoon or evening. Catered meals available by request. Smoking outside only.

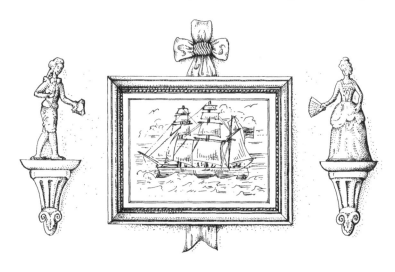

THE CHESHIRE CAT INN & COTTAGES
36 W Valerio St, 93101.

(805) 569-1610;
FAX (805) 682-1876

1P/1B   ...   2P/1B $ 99 - 300

XP $25. 3 pm check-in; noon check out. 2-night minimum stay weekends including Sat. Deposit required; 7-day refund notice; $15 cancellation fee.

An 1890 Queen Anne-style house with pagoda bay windows and an adjacent Victorian house feature antique furnishings, Laura Ashley decor and English gardens. The houses are located in a residential area near downtown. 14 rooms and suites, each with private bath; some units have whirlpool, balcony or fireplace; 3 cottages have private decks and hot tubs. Bicycles available for guests' use. No pets. AE, DI, MC, VI. Full breakfast served in the dining area, on the patio or in the guest room. Wine and hors d'oeuvres served daily 5-6 pm. In-room flowers and chocolate. Smoking outside only.

GLENBOROUGH INN
1327 Bath St, 93101.

(805) 966-0589, (800) 962-0589;
FAX (805) 564-8610

1P/1B $100 - 250   2P/1B $100 - 360   2P/2B $260 - 360

XP $30. 3-6 pm check-in; 11 am check out. 2-night minimum stay weekends. Deposit required.

3 historic homes contain antique furnishings and are set on spacious tree-shaded grounds in a residential area near downtown: an 1880s Victorian summer cottage, and 2 2-story California Craftsman houses dating from 1906 and 1912. 11 guest rooms, each with private bath; 3 suites with fireplace. In-room phone, coffeemaker; some with refrigerator. Private hot tub in the garden. No pets. AE, DI, DS, MC, VI. Full breakfast served in the garden or in guest rooms. Evening hors d'oeuvres and beverages served in the parlor. Smoking outside only.

INN ON SUMMER HILL
2520 Lillie Ave, Summerland 93067.

(805) 969-9998, (800) 845-5566;
FAX (805) 565-9946

1P/1B   ...   2P/1B $190 - 220   2P/2B $200
Suite $295

XP $25. 3 pm check-in; 11 am check out. 2-night minimum stay weekends and holidays. Deposit required; 7-day refund notice.

California Craftsman-style country inn with ocean-view rooms and antique furnishings is located 3 miles east of Santa Barbara. 16 guest rooms, each with private bath. Air conditioning; in-room gas fireplace, phone, TV with VCR, canopy bed, refrigerator and whirlpool tub. Outdoor whirlpool. No pets. AE, DS, MC, VI. Full breakfast served in the dining room. Afternoon tea and wine with hors d'oeuvres served in the dining room; evening desserts available. Smoking outside only.

THE MARY MAY INN
111 W Valerio St, 93101.

(805) 569-3398

1P/1B $100 - 180   2P/1B $100 - 180

XP $25. 3 pm check-in; 11 am check out. 2-night minimum stay weekends. Deposit required; 7-day refund notice; cancellation fee. Midweek discounts available.

Historical Queen Anne Victorian and Federal-style houses located 4 blocks from downtown date from the 1880s and feature gables, protruding bay windows, porches, patterned siding, turned woodwork and double-hung decorative windows. Interiors are elaborately detailed with hand-carved mantles and a mahogany grand staircase. 12 guest rooms, each with private bath, 4 with whirlpool tub, 4 with fireplace. Small pets allowed at innkeeper's discretion. AE, DS, MC, VI. Full breakfast served in dining room or on the patio. Late afternoon coffee and tea with sweets are served.

THE OLD YACHT CLUB INN
431 Corona del Mar Dr, 93103.

(805) 962-1277, (800) 549-1676 (California),
(800) 676-1676 (USA); FAX (805) 962-3989

1P/1B   ...   2P/1B $105 - 185

XP $30. 2 pm check-in; 11 am check out. 2-night minimum stay if including Sat. Deposit required; 7-day refund notice.

A 1912 Craftsman house with a central fireplace and covered porch is furnished with period pieces, European antiques and Oriental rugs; next-door the 1925 early California Spanish-style house contains antiques and Oriental rugs; both are located 1 block from the beach. 12 guest rooms, each with private bath. TV in some rooms upon request. Beach chairs and towels available for guests' use. No pets. AE, DI, MC, VI. Full breakfast served in the dining room. Wine served in the evening. Gourmet dinner usually served Sat; extra charge. Smoking outside only.

THE OLIVE HOUSE INN
1604 Olive St, 93101.

(805) 962-4902, (800) 786-6422;
FAX (805) 962-9983

1P/1B $110- 180   2P/1B $110 - 180

3-7 pm check-in; 11 am check out. 2-night minimum stay weekends; 3-night minimum on holidays. Deposit required; 7-day refund notice. Midweek discounts for 2-night stay, excluding holidays. Business rates.

A restored, 1904 Craftsman-style house features redwood paneling, bay windows and a fireplace in the living room. Ocean and mountain views, terraced garden, sun deck, private decks, hot tubs and fireplaces. Located in a residential neighborhood near the mission and downtown. 6 guest rooms, each with private bath. No pets. AE, DS, MC, VI. Full breakfast. Afternoon wine, evening tea and treats. Smoking outside only.

THE PARSONAGE
1600 Olive St, 93101.

(805) 962-9336, (800) 775-0352

1P/1B   ...   2P/1B $130 - 215   Suite $255 - 305

3 pm check-in; 11 am check out. 2-night minimum stay weekends. Deposit required; 7-day refund notice.

An 1892 Queen Anne Victorian house with Oriental rugs, stained glass, and antique furnishings is located in a residential area near Santa Barbara Mission. 6 guest rooms, each with private bath; a 3-room honeymoon suite has views of the city, mountains and ocean; some rooms have a fireplace and whirlpool tub. No pets. AE, DS, MC, VI. Full breakfast served in the dining room or on the sun deck. Afternoon refreshments. No smoking.

SECRET GARDEN INN & COTTAGES
1908 Bath St, 93101.

(805) 687-2300, (800) 676-1622;
FAX (805) 687-4576

1P/1B   ...   2P/1B $110 - 215   2P/2B $110 - 215

XP $20. 3-7 pm check-in; noon check out. 2-night minimum stay weekends and holidays. Deposit required; 7-day refund notice.

A 1915 California bungalow-style house and 4 adjacent cottages, located in a residential area near downtown, contain antique furnishings. 11 guest rooms, each with private bath. 5 2-room suites, 1 with fireplace and 4 with outdoor hot tubs. No pets. AE, DS, MC, VI. Full breakfast served in the dining room or on the patio. Evening refreshments include wine and hot spiced cider. Smoking outside only.

SIMPSON HOUSE INN
121 E Arrellaga St, 93101.

(805) 963-7067, (800) 676-1280;
FAX (805) 564-4811

1P/1B   ...   2P/1B $175 - 400

XP $25. 3 pm check-in; 11 am check out. 2-night minimum stay weekends. Deposit required; 7-day refund notice.

An 1874 Victorian estate with antique furnishings, fine art, patios and large verandas is situated in an acre of English gardens; located in a residential area near downtown. 14 cottages, suites and guest rooms, each with private bath. Some in-room fireplaces and whirlpools. Bicycles and English croquet sets available for guests' use. No pets. AE, DS, MC, VI. Full breakfast served in the dining area, on the veranda or private patios. Complimentary sherry and afternoon refreshments; wine, tea and Mediterranean hors d'oeuvres buffet served late in the day. Smoking outside only.

TIFFANY INN
1323 De la Vina St, 93101.

(805) 963-2283, (800) 999-5672;
FAX (805) 962-0994

1P/1B   ...   2P/1B $125- 225

3-7 pm check-in; 11 am check out. 2-night minimum stay weekends including Sat. Deposit required; 7-day refund notice.

An 1898, 3-story Colonial Revival house with diamond-pane bay windows, a porch and antique furnishings also boasts a Victorian-style garden. Located near downtown. 7 guest rooms with private bath, 5 with fireplace; 3 suites with whirlpool. No pets. AE, DS, MC, VI. Full breakfast served in the dining room. Evening beverages and hors d'oeuvres. Smoking outside only.

VILLA ROSA
15 Chapala St, 93101.

(805) 966-0851; FAX (805) 962-7159

1P/1B $100 - 250   2P/1B $100 - 250

3 pm check-in; noon check out. 2-night minimum stay required if Sat included. Deposit required; 5-day refund notice.

A contemporary Spanish Colonial hotel is within walking distance of the beach and Stearn's Wharf. 18 guest rooms, each with private bath. 4 rooms with fireplace and TV. In-room phone, evening turn-down service and morning newspaper. Pool, whirlpool. No pets. AE, MC, VI. Continental breakfast served in the dining area. Wine, cheese and fruit served in the afternoon; port or sherry offered in late evening. Smoking outside only.

❦ SANTA MONICA

CHANNEL ROAD INN   *(310) 459-1920; FAX (310) 454-9920*
219 W Channel Rd, 90402.

1P/1B   ...   2P/1B $125 - 275

3 pm check-in; noon check out. Deposit required; 3-day refund notice.

A 1910 Colonial Revival house furnished with period antiques is located 1 block from the beach in Santa Monica Canyon. 14 rooms, each with private bath; some rooms with fireplace, whirlpool or partial ocean view. In-room TV and phone. Outside whirlpool. Bicycles available for beach bike path. No pets. AE, MC, VI. Full breakfast served in the dining area. Wine and tea served in the afternoon.

❦ SANTA PAULA

THE FERN OAKS INN   *(805) 525-7747*
1025 Ojai Rd, 93060.

1P/1B   ...   2P/1B $ 95 - 110

3 pm check-in; noon check out. 2-night minimum stay on holidays. Deposit required; 7-day refund notice; $20 cancellation fee. Midweek rates.

Restored and elegantly furnished, a 2-story Spanish Revival house built in 1929 is located in the heart of Ventura County. Landscaped grounds include rose gardens and oak and citrus trees. 4 guest rooms, each with private bath. In-room fresh flowers and chocolates. Pool. No pets. Full gourmet breakfast served in a formal dining room. Complimentary gourmet cookies, fresh fruit, beverages and imported sherry available. Smoking outside only.

❦ SEAL BEACH

THE SEAL BEACH INN AND GARDENS *(562) 493-2416, (800) 443-3292;*
212 5th St, 90740. *FAX (562) 799-0483*

1P/1B ... 2P/1B $155 - 225

$10. 4 pm check-in; 11 am check out. Deposit required; 3-day refund notice.

A 1920s classic French Mediterranean-style country inn has a courtyard, fountains, antique statuary in the gardens and antique furnishings inside the inn. Located in a residential area 1 block from the beach. 23 guest rooms in cottages, courtyard rooms and suites, each with private bath. In-room TV and phone; fireplace in library. Pool. No pets. AE, DI, DS, MC, VI. Full breakfast served in the dining area. Complimentary cookies in each room. Smoking outside only.

❦ SOLVANG

THE BALLARD INN *(805) 688-7770, (800) 638-2466;*
2436 Baseline, Ballard 93463. *FAX (805) 688-9560*

1P/1B ... 2P/1B $170 - 250

3 pm check-in; noon check out. 2-night minimum stay weekends and holidays. Deposit required; 7-day refund notice.

A country inn decorated with local antiques and quilts is located near Solvang in the heart of Santa Barbara County's wine country. 15 guest rooms, each with private bath; 7 with fireplace. Air conditioning. No pets. AE, MC, VI. Full breakfast served in the dining room. Local wines and hors d'oeuvres served in the late afternoon. Dinner available Wed-Sun at Cafe Chardonnay.

STORYBOOK INN *(805) 688-1703, (800) 786-7925*
409 1st St, 93463.

1P/1B $ 99 - 189 2P/1B $ 99 - 189

XP $25. 3-9 pm check-in; noon check out. 2-night minimum stay weekends. Deposit required; 7-day refund notice. Lower rates weekdays.

An English Tudor-style house with balconies, patios, beveled leaded glass, and cobblestones has antique furnishings throughout. Each room is decorated in a Hans Christian Andersen story theme. 9 guest rooms, each with private bath; 2 with whirlpool tub. Most rooms with fireplace. In-room air conditioning. No pets. AE, DI, DS, MC, VI. Full breakfast Sat-Sun, continental breakfast Mon-Fri, served in the dining area; the gourmet kitchen has a restaurant. Beverage served in the evening. No smoking.

❦ SOUTH PASADENA

THE ARTIST'S INN
1038 Magnolia St, 91030.

(626) 799-5668, (888) 799-5668;
FAX (626) 799-3678

1P/1B	$100 - 170	2P/1B	$100 - 170	2P/2B	$100 - 170

XP $20. 3-6 pm check-in; noon check out. 2-night minimum stay weekends. Deposit required; 7-day refund notice; cancellation fee.

An 1895 Victorian-frame farmhouse with a spacious front porch and a 1909 cottage are surrounded by a white picket fence and a large rose garden. The house is decorated with antiques and fresh flowers, and each guest room reflects a different artist or art period: Degas, English, fauve, Gauguin, Georgia O'Keeffe, Grandma Moses, Italian, Impressionist and Van Gogh. 9 guest rooms, each with private bath. Suites available. Air conditioning; in-room TV upon request. 3 rooms have a whirlpool, 4 rooms have a fireplace. Croquet for guests' use. No pets. AE, MC, VI. Full breakfast served in the dining room or on the front porch. Afternoon tea and home-baked pastries are served at 4 pm. Smoking outside only.

THE BISSELL HOUSE BED & BREAKFAST
201 Orange Grove Ave, 91030.

(626) 441-3535;
FAX (626) 441-3671

1P/1B	$115 - 160	2P/1B	$115 - 160

2-night minimum stay weekends. Deposit required; 7-day refund notice.

Fully restored, 1887 Victorian house with leaded glass windows is furnished with antiques. Landscaped grounds are surrounded by a 40-foot hedge offering complete privacy. 5 guest rooms, each with private bath; 1 room with whirlpool tub. In-room air conditioning. Pool, whirlpool. No pets. In the dining area full breakfast is served Sat-Sun; expanded continental breakfast served Mon-Fri. Afternoon snack; beverages available all day. Smoking outside only.

🍎 SPRINGVILLE

ANNIE'S BED & BREAKFAST
33024 Globe Dr, 93265.

(559) 539-3827;
FAX (559) 539-2179

1P/1B	$ 85	2P/1B	$ 95	2P/2B	$ 95

XP $25. 3-6 pm check-in; 11 am check out. 2-night minimum stay holidays and special events. Deposit required; 15-day refund notice; $10 cancellation fee.

A 1903 country farmhouse and bunkhouse on 5 acres are decorated with antique furniture and handmade quilts. 3 guest rooms, each with private bath. Buildings are air cooled. Whirlpool, pool. Country club privileges nearby for golf and tennis. No pets. AE, DI, DS, MC, VI. Full breakfast cooked on a wood-burning stove and served in the dining room. Refreshments served in the afternoon. No smoking.

🍎 TEMECULA

LOMA VISTA BED AND BREAKFAST
33350 La Serena Wy, 92591.

(909) 676-7047;
FAX (909) 676-0077

1P/1B	...	2P/1B	$100 - 150

3-8 pm check-in; 11 am check out. Closed Dec 24-25. 2-night minimum stay weekends. Deposit required; 7-day refund notice.

Contemporary California Mission-style house located on a knoll overlooks a valley and vineyards. Located 5 miles east of town off Rancho California Road. 6 guest rooms, each with private bath; 4 with private balcony. Air conditioning. 2 large patios for guests' use, 1 with a fire pit and 1 with a whirlpool. No pets. MC, VI. Full champagne breakfast served family style in the dining room. Beverages and appetizers served in the early evening.

❦ TEMPLETON

COUNTRY HOUSE INN
91 Main St, 93465.

(805) 434-1598, (800) 362-6032

1P/1B $ 85 - 100   2P/1B $ 90 - 105

XP $15. 3 pm check-in; 11 am check out. 2-night minimum stay weekends. Deposit required; 7-day refund notice.

An 1886, 2-story Victorian house is surrounded by landscaped gardens and features antique furnishings; the house was built by the town's founder, C.H. Phillips. 5 guest rooms, each with private bath. No pets. DS, MC, VI. Full breakfast served in the dining area. No smoking.

❦ THREE RIVERS

ORGANIC GARDENS BED AND BREAKFAST
44095 Dinely Dr, 93271.

(559) 561-0916;
FAX (559) 561-1017

1P/1B $105   2P/1B $105

XP $25. 2 pm check-in; 10:30 am check out. 2-night minimum stay, 3-night minimum stay holidays. Credit card guarantee required; 7-day refund notice.

This cabin-style house on 5 acres has extensive decks and large windows with a view of the Sierra Nevada of Sequoia National Park. 2 guest rooms, each with private bath. Full breakfast served on deck in warm weather and inside main room in cool weather. Oranges or other seasonal fruit served upon arrival. In-room cooler, fan and fireplace. Hot tub. Organic gardens and art gallery. No pets. MC, VI. No smoking. Handicap accessible.

❦ TWENTYNINE PALMS

HOMESTEAD INN BED AND BREAKFAST
74153 Two Mile Rd, 92277.

(760) 367-0030;
FAX (760) 367-0030

1P/1B   ...   2P/1B $ 75 - 150

4 pm check-in; 11 am check out. Closed Jul 5 through Oct 1. 2-night minimum stay required on holiday weekends. Deposit required; 2-day refund notice.

A historic home built in 1928 has mahogany wood trim and is set on 15 acres that are attractive to local birds. Grounds include cactus gardens and tortoise habitat. The house is furnished with antiques and original art by local artists. 7 rooms, each with private bath. Arrangements can be made for horseback riding and for a massage therapist. No pets. AE, DS, MC, VI. Full breakfast served in the breakfast area. Smoking outside only.

THE K-B RANCHOTEL
6048 Noels Knoll Rd, 92277.

(760) 367-3353; FAX (760) 367-1554

1P/1B $ 45   2P/1B $ 55

XP $10. Closed Jun 28 through Sep 15, except by arrangement. 5-8 pm check-in; 2 pm check out. Reservation and deposit required; 7-day refund notice.

A large, historic adobe homestead built in 1935 is situated on 5 acres of high desert. Decorated with many original furnishings, the house also features 6 fireplaces, a walled courtyard with a fishpond and 2 cactus gardens on the grounds. 2 rooms, each with private bath and fireplace. Quiet hours 10 pm-6 am. Pets welcome by prior arrangement; $15 deposit. Continental breakfast served in the dining area. Afternoon snack consists of house specialties such as homemade salsa and chips or mesquite-smoked turkey. Smoking permitted in common areas.

THE ROUGHLEY MANOR
74744 Joe Davis Dr, 92277.

(760) 367-3238; FAX (760) 367-1690

1P/1B   ...   2P/1B $ 75 - 125

XP $25. 2 pm check-in; 11 am check out. Credit card guarantee; 2-day refund notice.

The 3-story main house, of Eastern design, was built in 1928 of native stone. It is situated on 25 acres; near the house are palm and cypress trees and a rose garden. 5 rooms with shared baths, 2 cottages with private baths. Central air conditioning and fireplaces in 2 bedrooms. Facilities for meetings and weddings. Pets allowed. AE, MC, VI. Full breakfast served in guest room or the great room. Evening tea and dessert. Smoking outside only.

TOWER HOMESTEAD BED AND BREAKFAST   *(760) 367-7936*
Amboy and Mojave rds; Box C141, 92277.

1P/1B $ 75   2P/1B $ 75

No specified check-in or check out times. Deposit required; 7-day refund notice.

Built in 1932 from a dismantled 100-year-old Pasadena house, the structure is part of a 160-acre homestead and contains desert flagstone patios and fireplace, pine paneling, functional antiques and desert landscaping. 2 bedrooms, each with living room and fireplace. Shared bath. TV. Spa. Barbecue facilities. No pets. Full breakfast served in the dining area or on the patio. Smoking permitted.

❧ VENICE

THE VENICE BEACH HOUSE   *(310) 823-1966; FAX (310) 823-1842*
15 30th Ave, 90291.

1P/1B   ...   2P/1B $ 95 - 165   2P/2B $ 95 - 130

XP $20. Deposit required; 5-day refund notice.

A 1911 California Craftsman home on the beach features a fireplace and veranda along with antique furnishings. 9 guest rooms, 5 with private bath. In-room phone and TV; 1 suite with hot tub, 1 suite with fireplace. No pets. AE, MC, VI. Full breakfast served in the dining area or on the veranda. Afternoon refreshments. Smoking outside only.

❦ VENTURA

ANCIENT AROMATICS AROMATHERAPY DAY SPA & GUEST SUITES
50 N Oak St, 93001.   *(805) 643-0609*

1P/1B   ...   2P/1B $105

4 pm check-in; 11 am check out. 2-night minimum stay on major holidays. Deposit required; 7-day refund notice; $15 cancellation fee. Corporate rates. Call for B&B/Spa packages.

A 1925 California Mission-style house features atriums, skylights, ornate tile and an arch. The house, close to old San Buenaventura shopping and the Pacific Ocean, was used as an artist's studio during the early 1900s. Each room is individually decorated. 3 guest rooms, each with private bath. Rooms are furnished with early 1900s antique furniture, antique bed and feather-filled mattress. Bathrooms provided with homemade natural soaps. 1 room with ocean view. No pets. MC, VI. Continental breakfast served in separate dining area. Smoking outside only.

BELLA MAGGIORE INN   *(805) 652-0277, (800) 523-8479 (California);*
67 S California St, 93001.   *FAX (805) 648-5670*

1P/1B $ 75 - 150   2P/1B $ 75 - 150

XP $10. 3 pm check-in; noon check out. Deposit required; 2-day refund notice.

A 1920s Northern Italian-style provincial inn designed by A. C. Martin, architect of Grauman's Chinese Theater and the Los Angeles City Hall, is located in the old downtown business district near Mission San Buenaventura and the beach. 24 rooms and suites; all with private bath, in-room phone and TV; some with whirlpool, fireplace or bay window and/or air conditioning. No pets. AE, DI, DS, MC, VI. Fine dining on premises. Full breakfast served in the dining room or courtyard. Afternoon appetizers and beverages. Some rooms for smokers.

LA MER   *(805) 643-3600; FAX (805) 653-7329*
411 Poli St, 93001.

1P/1B $ 80 - 175   2P/1B $ 90 - 185

4 pm check-in; noon check out. 2-night minimum stay weekends. Deposit required; 7-day refund notice. Midweek rates.

An 1890 Cape Cod-Victorian house is filled with antiques, each room representing a particular European country. The house is situated on a hillside overlooking old San Buenaventura and the Pacific Ocean. 5 guest rooms, each with private bath. 1 room with fireplace; 4 rooms with private entrance. Remote phone upon request. No pets. AE, MC, VI. Expanded Bavarian buffet-style breakfast served in the breakfast room. Complimentary champagne, wine or sparkling cider upon arrival. Smoking outside only.

❦ VISALIA

BEN MADDOX HOUSE   *(559) 739-0721, (800) 401-9800*
601 N Encina St, 93291.

1P/1B $ 80   2P/1B $ 95

3 pm check-in; 11 am check out. Deposit required; 3-day refund notice.

This restored house, built in 1876, has Greek columns and front and side porches; it was the home of pioneer Ben Maddox. The house is located close to downtown in a residential area of historical homes. 4 guest rooms, each with private bath. In-room air conditioning, TV and phone. Pool and hot tub. No pets. AE, DS, MC, VI. Full breakfast served in separate dining area or on deck. Beverages and snacks. Smoking outside only.

END OF THE RAINBOW   *(559) 594-4499*
18344 Ave 304, 93292.

1P/1B $ 75   2P/1B $ 85   2P/2B $ 85

XP $15. 4 pm check-in; 11 am check out. Deposit required; 7-day refund notice; $10 cancellation charge.

Contemporary 2-story Colonial house surrounded by oak trees sits on a 35-acre ranch 10 miles east of Visalia, en route to 2 national parks. 2 guest rooms with 2 shared baths; 1 room can sleep up to 5 persons. Decks for sunbathing. TV in common room; in-room TV available. Walking trail along Kaweah River. Private pasture and overnight boarding for travelers with horses. No pets allowed. Full breakfast served in dining room or on porch. Afternoon beverages and homemade pastries. No smoking.

THE SPALDING HOUSE   *(559) 739-7877; FAX (559) 625-0902*
631 N Encina St, 93291.

1P/1B $ 75   2P/1B $ 85

No specified check-in or check out times. Deposit required; 48-hour refund notice.

A 1901 Colonial Revival-style house is decorated with many antiques and features handcrafted beveled glass doors, a library and a music room with a 1923 Steinway grand player piano. The house is located in a residential area of historical homes. 3 guest rooms, each with private bath and sitting room. Full breakfast served in the dining room. No pets. MC, VI. Afternoon refreshments. Smoking outside only.

❦ WOODLAKE

WICKY-UP RANCH BED & BREAKFAST   *(559) 564-8898*
22702 Ave 344, 93286.

1P/1B $ 85   2P/1B $ 90

3 pm check-in; 11 am check out. Deposit required; 7-day refund notice, (14-day for holidays); full refund if room re-rented.

Built in 1902, this California Craftsman-style house has been in the same family for 5 generations. Surrounded by orange trees in a rural setting near Sequoia National Park, the house features antiques, original paintings, Oriental rugs and unique woodwork. One guest room with private bath, Victorian bed, fireplace, living room and veranda. Video library. No pets. Full breakfast served in separate dining area. Afternoon refreshments. Smoking outside only.

❦ WRIGHTWOOD

OGILVIE MANOR   *(760) 249-6537*
1894 Ash Rd; Box 475, 92397.

1P/1B $100   2P/1B $100

XP $25. 2 pm check-in; 10:30 am check out. 2-night minimum stay required on holidays. Deposit required; 3-day refund notice.

Tudor-style house with English country decor has a library with fireplace. Immaculate gardens and lawns surround the manor house in a mountain setting. 3-room suite and 2-room detached guest house, each with private bath. Guest rooms have TV with VCR. No pets. Expanded continental breakfast served in the guest room or dining room. Afternoon tea. Smoking outside only.

Appendices

Reservations and Referral Agencies

The following list is an additional resource for those requiring more information or a larger selection of B&B-style accommodations. These agencies offer services on behalf of inns and private homes (commonly known as homestays) that provide rooms appealing to the bed and breakfast traveler. Some agencies inspect the facilities they recommend, while others do not. Services vary with each organization. Some place reservations, while others will provide a name of an accommodation to contact or mail a list of facilities. Charges vary and should be discussed with each service provider before arrangements are finalized.

BED & BREAKFAST 800 *(800) 424-0053*
1027 N Coast Hwy, Ste A, Laguna Beach 92651.
Reservation Area: California Coast.

BED & BREAKFAST CALIFORNIA *(650) 696-1690, (800) 872-4500;*
PO Box 282910, San Francisco 94128-2910. *FAX (650) 696-1699*
Reservation Areas: California, Nevada.

BED & BREAKFAST HOMESTAY *(805) 927-4613*
PO Box 326, Cambria 93428.
Reservation Area: Cambria.

BED & BREAKFAST SAN FRANCISCO *(415) 479-1913*
PO Box 420009, San Francisco 94142.
Reservation Areas: Metro San Francisco Area, Marin, Wine Country, Yosemite, Monterey, Carmel.

CALIFORNIA ASSOCIATION OF *(831) 464-8159, (800) 284-4667;*
BED & BREAKFAST INNS *FAX (831) 462-0402*
2715 Porter St, Soquel 95073.
Reservation Area: California.

CENTRAL COAST RESERVATIONS *(805) 898-1905, (800) 557-7898*
PO Box 3086, Santa Barbara 93130.
Reservation Areas: Santa Barbara, San Luis Obispo and Ventura counties.

MEGAN'S FRIENDS *(805) 544-4406*
1776 Royal Wy, San Luis Obispo 93405.
Reservation Areas: San Luis Obispo and Santa Barbara counties.

WINE COUNTRY RESERVATIONS *(707) 257-7757, 944-1109*
PO Box 5059, Napa 94581.
Reservation Areas: Napa and Sonoma counties.

Index to Bed and Breakfast Inns